D0044194

VIEWPOINTS

Fresh Perspectives
on Personal Support Raising

STEVE SHADRACH

CMM PRESS

CMM Press is the publishing ministry of the Center for Mission Mobilization (CMM), an international Christian ministry.

Support Raising Solutions is a ministry of the CMM that is dedicated to flooding the nations with spiritually healthy, vision-driven, fully funded, Great Commission workers.

For more resources, go to cmmpress.org or supportraisingsolutions.org.

Viewpoints
by Steve Shadrach

© 2010, by Steve Shadrach

ISBN-13: 978-0-9825107-0-4

CMM Press
PO Box 3556
Fayetteville, AR 72702
www.cmmpress.org

Printed in the United States of America
2nd Printing, 2014

Unless otherwise identified, all Scripture quotations are taken from the New American Standard Bible®, Copyright © 1960, 1962, 1963, 1968, 1971, 1972, 1973, 1975, 1977, 1995 by The Lockman Foundation Used by permission. www.Lockman.org

OTHER CHRISTIAN LEADERS WEIGH IN

"This series of practical answers to on-the-ground questions about fundraising ought to be in every Christian worker's library. Besides answering my questions, the articles inspire me not only in fundraising but also in leadership."

Scott Morton
Vice-President of Development for The Navigators
Author of *Funding Your Ministry: Whether Your're Gifted or Not*

"Fully funded" is a declaration of God's abundant provision for the Christian worker. In *Viewpoints*, Steve Shadrach captures simple yet profound support-raising principles leading to that declaration of "fully funded." The staff at Crown benefit tremendously from learning and employing these principles. Whether you are a support raiser or a supporter, these short chapters contain nuggets of wisdom that will allow the declaration of "fully funded" to ring loudly throughout teams of Christian ministry workers around the world."

Sharon Epps
Partner and Consultant for Women Doing Well

"Steve Shadrach's *Viewpoints* is brimming with practical helps for support raising as well as great encouragement. His experiences from many years of living on missionary support gives rich wisdom and perspective on a vast array of topics and concerns. Whatever you're struggling with regarding support raising, you'll find help in this book!"

Betty Barnett
YWAM missionary and author of *Friend Raising: Builing A Missionary Support Team That Lasts*

"*Viewpoints: Fresh Perspectives on Personal Support Raising* is a strategic evaluation of missionary personal support raising. I believe this should be read by every person involved in support raising, from the new missionary in the midst of support raising, including all of those in the chain of involvement right up to the CEO of the mission agency. Steve writes in a very organized, direct, to-the-point manner addressing all the basic questions one might raise concerning personal support raising. The reader will find it refreshing, enlightening, and, for the one in the midst of such support raising, of great encouragement! Truly a resourceful handbook on personal support raising."

John E. Kyle
Former Wycliffe Bible Translators missionary; Executive Director, Mission To The World — PCA;
Missions and Urbana Director, Vice President — IVCF;
Senior Vice President, Evangelical Fellowship of Mission Agencies

"From years of experience, Steve Shadrach has compiled a practical and comprehensive volume on personal support raising. If you apply these principles, I'm confident you will see God provide more Kingdom resources in less time."

Steve Moore
President and CEO, Missio Nexus

"Steve covers every cause I can think of related to donor relations and support raising. He not only covers all the many facets in this book, he also covers them from God's perspective — a 'must read' even for the experienced."

John Maisel
Founder, East-West Ministries International

"*Viewpoints* captures the core principles and practices necessary for developing a committed team of people to pray for and support your ministry calling. You will not likely agree with everything in this book, but you will be challenged to think more deeply and pray more diligently as you pursue what God has for His best for you in this arena. Those new to developing a ministry team of supporters will be stimulated by each of the short chapters in this book. Those already blessed by a team of supporters should read a chapter a week to keep your mind full of ideas, praise on your lips for your individual team members, and prayer for new people to join in the effort."

Greg Parsons
Global Director, U.S. Center for World Mission

"Fundraising is hard work and frequently feels like an uphill climb. However, the view from the top can transform all the effort into blessing. In *Viewpoints*, Steve Shadrach offers biblical perspectives, practical suggestions and wise counsel on raising support that is born out of years of spending time on the mountain. I encourage you to let him be your guide, whether you are just starting your fundraising journey or are a veteran climber!"

Donna Wilson
National Director of Training for Staff MPD, InterVarsity Christian Fellowship/USA

"Many people see support raising as a wall with a moat on the other side. It represents the barrier to get over in order to get to 'real ministry.' Some can scale the wall or help others scale the wall, but I truly believe God has raised up Steve Shadrach in our day to be a part of bringing the wall down — thus unleashing myriads of laborers into the world. *Viewpoints* will help you and your staff tear down the various walls in your own mind — like fear, lack of training, and small vision. My staff and I personally are indebted to Steve for these biblical and relevant insights. The greatest discovery you will make is that the very wall that has fallen is actually the bridge that God has placed there to carry you to where you need to be."

Claude Hickman
National Director, The Traveling Team

"Steve Shadrach's insights and challenges run against the quick-fix, mass-mailing, email-appeal, shallow-relationship approaches that characterize much of the support raising that takes place today. Such methods often leave people disappointed and frustrated and produce little or no support. But if you are eager to work hard to develop a solid, faithful support team to undergird your ministry, then this book is for you. Be warned in advance, *Viewpoints* challenges you with a very high bar. It is filled with encouraging case studies and anecdotes that will leave you with the sense that 'I CAN DO THIS!' Plowing, cultivating, planting, and weeding are all arduous tasks, but the Lord does not bring forth a harvest without them."

Dave Flynn
Former National Director, Perspectives on the World Christian Movement Study Program

"Fundraising is ministry! One doesn't have to be around Steve Shadrach very long to know that Steve practices what he preaches. I would highly recommend *Viewpoints* as a practical ministry textbook that tackles many of the hard questions, describes the necessary attitudes, and addresses strategic topics that are common to fundraisers. May God use *Viewpoints* to grow His Kingdom."

Ken Rudeen
Leader of Ministry Partner Development Greater Europe Mission

VIEWPOINTS

ACKNOWLEDGMENTS

Thanks to all of the people who contributed to the articles on the SRS Blog. I am grateful.

Thanks to Stephen Caldwell and his WordBuilders Communications team for shepherding this book through the entire process from A to Z. Great job!

Thanks to Laura Lacy, Megan Barr, Meredith Erhard, Clay Bell, John Patton, and Carol Shadrach for their proofing, helpful input, and critique. Honesty is always the best policy!

Thanks to Darren Huckey and MonstorGraphix.com for the awesome graphic design work on this project and so many others over the years. You are one creative dude!

Thanks to the board of directors of The Center for Mission Mobilization for believing in this vision and launching a new publishing arm: CMM Press. Let's trust God to produce many more life-changing, world-changing tools and resources for the body of Christ.

Finally, thanks to Scott Morton with the Navigators, Ellis Goldstein with Cru, Donna Wilson with InterVarsity, and Betty Barnett with YWAM for your encouragement and friendship. You four, and so many others, have pioneered and paved the way for young bucks like myself. You are my heroes.

CONTRIBUTORS TO THE
SRS NEWSLETTER

Scott Morton	The Navigators
David Dougherty	OMF International
Henri Moreau	Chi Alpha
Ellis Goldstein	Cru
Steve Doggett	EFCA ReachGlobal
Jamie Hanson	Young Life
Mike Jorgensen	e3 Partners
Donna Wilson	InterVarsity Christian Fellowship
Scott Gore	Frontiers Mission Agency
Bill Dillon	PeopleRaising.com
Doug Bozung	Greater Europe Mission
Holmes Bryan	Evangelical Development Ministry
Dave English	Global Opportunities Ministry
Richard Beach	Doulos Ministries
Tim Freeman	GlobeServe
Jim Dempsey	Cru
Jim Topmiller	Cru
Jim Raymo	WEC International
Greg Parsons	U.S. Center for World Mission
Sharon Epps	Crown Financial Ministries
John Maisel	East West Ministries
David Armstrong	Mission Data International
Stephen Caldwell	WordBuilders Communications
Tim Biscaye	Caleb Project
Dr. Art Deyo	Youth For Christ
Pam Nolen	Fellowship Bible Church of Northwest Arkansas
Dr. Mike Bickley	Olathe Bible Church (Kansas)
Matt Pace	Student Mobilization
John Ray	YWAM
Kelvin Wyrick	Wyrick Law Firm, Texarkana, Texas
John Kyle	Wycliffe/InterVarsity/EFMA

Dr. Greg Fritz	Partners International
Darryl Cedergren	Mission Aviation Fellowship
Dale Losch	Crossworld
Chuck Schwaninger	Cru
Ken Wilson	Fellowship Bible Church of Conway, Arkansas
Ken Rudeen	Greater Europe Mission
Pat Kershaw	International Students, Inc.
Bill Glidden	American Missionary Fellowship
Ray Zuercher	YouthFront
Jean Wunsch	Mission Aviation Fellowship
Gene Van Den Bosch	EFCA ReachGlobal
George Loring	Missions Door
Rory Brannum	Entrepreneur/Missionary to Middle East
Fouad Masri	Crescent Project
Dave Flynn	Perspectives Study Program
Jeff Anderson	Crown Financial Ministries
Brent Eimer	MinistryHome
Dick Nelson	Fellowship Bible Church of Northwest Arkansas
John Maxwell	Author/Leadership Expert
Dave Meyers	New Tribes Mission
David Auterson	Assembly of God
Dave Ramsey	DaveRamsey.com
Jeff Shackelford	American Missionary Fellowship

TABLE OF CONTENTS

SECTION I: FIVE PARADIGMS TO EMBRACE

SECTION II: SEVEN CONVICTIONS TO ABSORB

SECTION III: EIGHT ATTITUDES TO RADIATE

SECTION IV: EIGHT QUESTIONS TO ASK

SECTION V: SIX RELATIONSHIPS TO NURTURE

SECTION VI: FIVE STRATEGIES TO FOLLOW

SECTION VII: NINE ISSUES FOR LEADERS TO EXAMINE

SECTION VIII: NINE 'SECOND OPINIONS' TO ASSESS

SECTION IX: EIGHT BONUS FEATURES TO PERUSE

FOREWORD

BY ELLIS GOLDSTEIN

National Director of Ministry Partner Development for Cru, the U.S. ministry of Campus Crusade for Christ

Missionaries are some of the most courageous people I have ever met. Over the years, I have had the privilege of training thousands of these men and women who have counted the cost so that they can follow the Lord's call for their lives. They are some of the boldest people you will ever meet and are deeply committed to helping fulfill the Great Commission.

Yet while they would never hesitate to tell someone about God's love and forgiveness, having to ask someone to support their ministry causes many to quake in their boots. Why is that? Why is there such a struggle to ask people to give? There are many reasons, but at the heart of it is a simple question each missionary needs to ask: "Am I raising money for myself or am I inviting people to use their financial resources to join with the God of all Creation in His vision to reach the lost?"

God has entrusted every one of His children with some of His infinite resources. For those who raise support, we have a profound and sacred responsibility to encourage generous giving. King David understood this. In I Chronicles 28-29 he passes the torch to his son Solomon for the building of the Temple. All of his officials are present and he asks them this question, "Now, who is willing to consecrate himself today to the Lord?" They understood exactly what he was asking. With a very willing heart they responded by giving generously for the building of the Temple. Through their giving they were connected to the very heart of God.

That's the privilege that anyone who raises support has — connecting people to the heart of God. Steve Shadrach understands this very well. He has helped thousands of missionaries take the steps of faith needed to overcome their fears in raising support. In the pages that follow you will find practical answers for most of the questions Christian workers have ever asked about raising support. Not only that, but your personal faith will be challenged to grow and trust God in greater ways for His provision for your ministry.

INTRODUCTION

Dear friend,

With this book we are attempting to influence the influencers, and, yes, you are one. You have taken two huge steps of faith: The first was following God's calling into full-time ministry. The second, though, may be even greater — the decision to take on the task of raising your personal financial support. And for that reason alone, I respect you immensely. Having lived and ministered on support myself since 1986, I count it a privilege to stand with you as a fellow support raiser, knowing the sacrifices you have made to see your team become a reality. I know it is a "God thing" and it is He who put all the pieces together, but the Lord did use you to do it!

There are a lot of books and seminars out there on how to do *major donor* fundraising. Some of the principles are the same, but understand the difference — here we are focusing exclusively on the issues, questions, and strategies *individual* Christian workers deal with as they *personally* invite family, friends, acquaintances, churches, etc., to join their *monthly* support team.

We struggled on what to name this book. Some suggested *PowerPoints*, but it sounded too much like a computer program. Others thought *Root to Fruit* would convey the cause and effects of good (or bad) paradigms. A few even wanted to title it *Shad-o-nomics* to reflect the financial philosophies of the author. My ego was stroked by the idea, but I squashed it as just a tad too corny. Finally, the simple name *Viewpoints* with the subtitle *Fresh Perspectives on Personal Support Raising* won out. Why? Because these 65 chapters mostly contain just opinions, thoughts, and suggestions you must evaluate for *yourself*.

So, be an Acts 17:11 believer who carefully soaks in all that is taught, but then immediately goes home and compares it to the Word of God. I would not expect you to agree with everything in this book, but my hope is that it will stimulate you to think, pray, study, and determine what you believe and what action you will take as a result.

One thing we can agree on: Starting from scratch and raising your entire support is similar to climbing a tall mountain. The journey to the top can be full of twists and turns, victories and defeats, aches and pains, tears of sorrow and finally … joy! We want to be there to offer you a helping hand to get to the top.

Let me slip in a few disclaimers. Most of the stories are true accounts of real people, but there are a few "composite characters" created from the reams of people and scenarios we have dealt with over the years. Also, even though I believe biblical principles are trans-cultural, the particular philosophy and approaches we promote in this book are primarily applicable to the majority culture here in the West. If you are an ethnic minority or from another part of the world, you may have to adjust this information to fit your cultural context.

Lastly, if you enjoy reading this volume, grab a copy of the companion book entitled *The God Ask*. If *Viewpoints* takes a broader macro look at support raising focused on the what's and the why's, then this longer second book takes a much more detailed micro look at support raising, focusing mainly on all the how to's of putting your team together. Hope you will order copies of *both* books for *all* the Christian workers you know who raise their own support.

As I write this, I am praying (in advance!) that you will sense and see God's blessings on your life and ministry and support raising — and that I might have a small part in providing some assistance along the way.

Warmly,

Steve Shadrach
Fayetteville, Arkansas

Section I

Five Paradigms to Embrace

FOLLOWERSHIP

Jesus really did live on support!

Soon afterwards, He began going around from one city and village to another, proclaiming and preaching the kingdom of God. The twelve were with Him, and also some women who had been healed of evil spirits and sicknesses: Mary who was called Magdalene, from whom seven demons had gone out, and Joanna the wife of Chuza, Herod's steward, and Susanna, and many others who were contributing to their support out of their private means. — Luke 8:1-3

This is unbelievable. It's hard enough to imagine the Son of God, King of kings and Lord of lords, lowering Himself from the glories of heaven for 33 years to get His hands dirty among us mere mortals. But are we also to understand that He then actually *chose* to totally rely on other earthlings for His very sustenance? You've got to be kidding!

This money Jesus and His men received wasn't from the church budget, foundations, or even major donor "sugar daddies." No, it was regular, ongoing support from *individuals*. Yes, He could have done it differently and outfitted His guys with moneychangers on each hip — *cha-ching*, and out shoots the gold coins. That would have drawn a crowd! So, *why* would the omnipotent God (who could snap His finger and have trillions of dollars at His feet) pick this method of funding?

1. JESUS WAS INTO *INTER*DEPENDENCE

He wanted to initiate and experience a simultaneous dependence upon God *and* those around Him. He was launching the mysterious interconnected network called the "Body of Christ" in which we look to both God *and* each other. He designed it — let's enjoy it!

2. JESUS WAS MODELING TO HIS MEN

Everything He ever did was partly so we could learn how to do it ourselves. Just two chapters later (Luke 10:1-8) Jesus sends His men out in pairs to ask for support and do ministry. When they found a willing investor, He charged them to "Stay in that house, eating and drinking what they give you; for the laborer is worthy of his wages. Do not keep moving from house to house." (v.7). The Lord wanted them to ask individuals (even ones they didn't know!) for support. He was onto something: Even today, right at 75 percent of all the U.S. charitable giving comes from individuals. The rest comes mostly from corporations, foundations, and bequeaths.

3. JESUS LOVED TO DO THINGS THE 'UN-WORLDLY' WAY

Whether it's our salvation or ministry funding, our natural inclination usually is this: Only by earning it ourselves can we truly deserve it. In our SRS Bootcamps, we ask the 50 or so participants how many have parents who were thrilled they were going into full-time ministry and raising their support. Only two or three usually raise their hands. The rest have parents who are wondering why their kid doesn't get a real job, work hard, and make his own way in life instead of freeloading on God and other poor souls who have enough financial pressures without someone asking them to cough up more! I know it feels so "un-American," but WWJD? Obviously, minister and live on the support of others.

2

FULFILLMENT

{ 'It is more blessed to give than to receive' }

Some Christian workers view support-raising as a feel-good movie with a happy ending, while others see it more like a horror film — maybe a combination of The Perfect Storm and Jaws! For them, living on support is like being lost at sea in a tiny lifeboat that's ravaged by huge killer waves, about to be thrown overboard any moment. And instead of seeing potential givers as friends and ministry partners, they eye them with fear and suspicion — as if they were circling, blood-thirsty sharks anxious to devour them. Wow. Can you say "paranoia"?

But for most of us perception is reality, and how we view circumstances and people can make us or break us. Instead of smiling at the future and believing the best in people (rather than the worst!), we can allow pessimism and excuses to thwart our support-raising success. "Attitude is everything," says author Charles Swindoll, adding that just 10 percent of life is what actually happens to us, while a whopping 90 percent is how we respond to it! So turn in your Bibles, if you would, to today's scripture reading — Acts 20:35, where Paul quotes Jesus:

"It is more blessed to give than to receive."

Skeptics may question the veracity of that verse because there's no place in the Gospels where the Lord makes this statement. A few cynics might even claim Paul conjured up that quote because he was in the middle of a church-building project or budget deficit and needed a proof text for his sermon on tithing! Still others, who absolutely love getting presents on holidays and birthdays, suspect Luke (the author of Acts) got confused and surely meant to write, "receiving is much better than giving."

Or maybe this verse is Jesus once again taking secret pleasure in shocking us with bold proclamations that rearrange the circuits in our puny brains. He delights in switching the price tags — forcing us to grapple with and choose between what the world values and what God esteems. Of course, the most scientific method to bring resolution to any research question is to "Google it" and see what pops up. Knowing Google is where this generation turns for answers, I typed in "better to give than receive." It returned an overwhelming 120,000 links, while the phrase "better to receive than give" brought up a measly 982! Proof positive, right? If not, maybe these ponderings will help:

1. GOD IS A GIVER

To understand this point, look no further than Romans 8:32-33: "He who did not spare his own Son, but gave Him up for us all — how will He not also, along with Him, graciously give us all things?" Just as parents derive great joy in giving gifts to their children, so our heavenly Father delights in lavishly pouring out His blessings of grace upon us.

2. GOD MADE US TO BE GIVERS

In spite of our depravity, man was made in the image of God, thus possessing portions (or traces) of His character. As a result, our Creator placed within every human an innate desire to give. Satan severely damages this predisposition by constantly wooing us away from selflessness to selfishness. We may question the motives of an Oprah or a Bono, but they continue to reach out because they've experienced the blessing of giving. Maybe I'm just an eternal optimist, but I propose we give each individual the benefit of the doubt and view everyone as a "giver," extending to them the opportunity to go beyond themselves and exercise this God-ordained characteristic.

3. GIVING PRODUCES HAPPINESS

My pastor teaches the word blessed means "oh the happiness of" and that Jesus is communicating in this verse that the simple act of giving will produce in any person a joy and satisfaction that receiving never can. If you will commit your life to asking others to give, you'll be partnering with God to help those around you fulfill their purpose and destiny in life. You've been blessed; now pass on the blessings!

Bottom line: Satan will whisper in your ear, "People are busy. They don't want to give. Times are tough. Leave them alone. Don't ask."

Instead, listen to Jesus: "It is more blessed to give than to receive."

3

STABILITY

The most 'secure' job you'll ever have

J ack felt sure numerous top-tier job offers would arrive at his door
now that he had completed his MBA. He had worked so hard
packing his resume with good grades, service activities, previous
jobs and internships, and, of course, an all-star cast of references. He
also was secretly counting on his network of fraternity brothers and his
Tom Cruise good looks as "icing on the cake."

When no great offers came forth, he aggressively hit the phones
and streets in pursuit of his fast track to the top. A tad embarrassed,
he accepted a low-level sales job. He knew he could prove himself,
but six months later the company was bought out and his department
was eliminated. Back in the hunt, he found another position in a
different state that lasted 18 months before the economy forced them
to cut back, too.

Twelve years later, Jack felt like a rag doll being jerked in every
direction. He had tried real estate, insurance, even day trading
thinking he would hit his jackpot any day. His quest for the
comfortable and secure "American dream" had morphed into a
nightmare of financial stress for him and his now burgeoning family.

Jack's story is not unlike the multitude of men and women who live
and work near us — and sometimes even support us! They *believed*
their college degree, hard work, and the supposedly unbreakable U.S.
economy would guarantee long-term stability. Decades later, feeling
beaten and betrayed, they would laugh aloud at the concept of "job
security," declaring it to be a mirage.

I've been offered several jobs during my years of living and
ministering on support, including one that paid four times what I was
making. It flabbergasted my dad that I wouldn't even consider the
position (read: big salary), but instead chose to labor on with my

seemingly small and fixed level of support. What my businessman father didn't understand was that I, in fact, held the most secure job on the planet.

Don't get me wrong: Our security and stability come from God, and God alone. But humanly speaking, that esteemed executive position with a corner office, silver nameplate, and six-digit salary is like the fescue seed I scattered in my yard yesterday. It can vanish at the first wisp of a wind! But I feel totally different about my support team.

Consider this: God has given me 60 monthly (and 30 annual) supporters who live in different parts of the country and work in various sectors of the economy. Similar to a stockbroker's advice, it's wise to have a diversified "portfolio." If the economy is hammering my Northeast supporters, my West Coast givers probably are doing better and want to share. If my donors in banking need to cut back for a year or two, my partners in the energy industry may be pouring extra funds into my account.

APPLICATION NO. 1

If you simply appreciate and communicate with your supporters over the long haul, they will stick with you through thick and thin, whether you are with the same organization or move to another.

APPLICATION NO. 2

Do you know people who hesitate to make the *jump* from their "secure" secular job and monthly paycheck to join your ministry and raise their "unsecured" support? Help them rethink their perspective. Taking that step may be the most stable, steady, secure thing they've ever done!

URGENCY

100 percent in 100 days? You must be kidding!

We conducted an informal survey of around 100 mission agencies at a recent Urbana Missions Conference in Illinois. Our interviewers went from booth to booth asking, "What is the average amount of time it takes your missionaries to raise their full support?" The average: 23 months!

When I share that shocking figure in our seminars around the country, I then ask the question: "Would you like to spend the next 23 months of your life raising support?"

The answer is always a resounding NO!

Who's responsible for creating these self-imposed support raising marathons? It often begins when the newly accepted missionary innocently asks his supervisor: "How long does it usually take someone to raise all his support?" The seasoned veteran then casually responds, "Oh, about 18 months." With that time frame now cemented in his psyche, the rookie staffer sets out to pace himself, making sure that he dare not deviate from "the norm."

So I shock more than a few people when I suggest they can get to 100 percent in 100 days. That's no gimmick. When Nehemiah asked King Artaxerxes how long it would take him to complete his Jerusalem rebuilding project, the trusted servant gave his boss a "definite time." If Nehemiah had just said, "Oh, it will be finished whenever the Lord leads," I have a feeling the King would not have been impressed. (Note: Nehemiah pulled it off in 52 days).

But setting a support-raising completion date of as little as 100 days should come with five pre-requisites. The Christian worker must:

1. Obtain the right training
2. Gain the right perspective

3. Use the right approach (there are a number of good approaches, although most workers don't even have one!)

4. Secure the right accountability

5. Focus on it FULL-TIME

Mixed with a ton of hard work and the blessings of God, I believe most workers can raise their support in three to six months.

And instead of key supporters giving $100, $200, or $300 a month, a number of them should make a bigger step of faith by writing an initial "launching" check of $1,000, $2,500, $4,000, or more. This buys the support raiser a "window of opportunity" to pray and work like never before, seeking three to five appointments a day (while still paying the bills and financing support-raising efforts). This "sprint approach" also produces a UQ (Urgency Quotient) that far surpasses the typical part-time, slow-moving 18-23 month support-raising walkathon.

I believe God wants all Christian workers engaged in their assignment quickly — and fully funded. Is 100 percent in 100 days impossible? My Bible says nothing is impossible — with God.

NOTE: *Just as I've seen people "sandbag" and pad their estimate of how long it will take to raise support, I also have known people who have gone in the other ditch and claimed they were going to put their team together in two weeks! As for you: Through prayer and experienced counsel, set reasonable but challenging start and finish dates.*

5

RISK

Support raising might just 'ruin' your life

One of my responsibilities is to help oversee the study program Perspectives on the World Christian Movement. This 15-week class in more than 210 locations around the U.S. (plus 27 countries) helps lay people, students (and yes, even Christian workers) understand God's heart for the nations and their most strategic role in completing the Great Commission.

Over the years, as I interact with a number of our 80,000-plus alumni, I've heard them say, "Perspectives ruined my life!" Normally, I would grieve and console them, but they offered their statement with a smile on their face and joy in their heart! When I probe deeper, they declare they're finished living a self-centered and mediocre Christian life — now and forever "ruined" for the ordinary. They want to trade in their puny little agenda and goals in order to fully give themselves to God's glory among the nations.

The more I observe the life-altering, paradigm-shifting experience people (like me!) have had with Perspectives, the more I see how the decision to raise our own personal support can have a similar effect. If and when we step out in faith to fund ourselves and our ministries, here are three ways it might just "ruin" our life:

1. MOVES US FROM SECURITY TO SIGNIFICANCE

John Eldredge, in his little book *Dare to Desire*, says, "God has rigged the world so that it only works when we embrace risk as the theme of our lives. ... All attempts to find a safer life, to live by the expectations of others, just kills the soul in the end. That's not how we find life." Eldredge then challenges us to choose a path of eternal significance rather than over-analyzing and feeling the need to always take the most secure route. He says, "Don't ask HOW — that will cut your desire off at the knees. HOW is never the right question. HOW is a faithless question. It means 'unless I can see my way clearly I won't venture forth.'" For me, making the decision to go into ministry and raise my full support broke me out of my old and hardened ways of thinking, helped me walk toward my fears, and prodded me to ask bigger questions than just "how can I keep from failing?"

2. SETS THE PATTERN FOR OTHER AREAS OF LIFE

Like the building of a skyscraper, taking on the monumental challenge of raising your total support from scratch can become a cornerstone that shapes all other pursuits — launching a life-long pattern of picking the road less traveled. Whether it is choices dealing with your relationship with God or spouse, location or vocation, personal or financial decisions, you are building a track record of hard, but faith-filled decisions that set the course for your entire life. Never underestimate how these early and seemingly small steps of faith can have a profound effect on how our life and legacy turns out 30, 40, 50 years from now.

3. EXPOSES THE BAGGAGE CLOGGING OUR HEARTS AND MINDS

Donna Wilson with InterVarsity has some insights regarding how engaging in the whole process of support raising can dredge up all kinds of junk from our past. At first glance, this may *seem* destructive, but anything that helps us identify and deal with prior hurts and wounds ultimately makes us healthier, stronger, more able to love and minister — and raise support! So, when the funnel cloud of support raising comes crashing through threatening to depress or enslave you, don't run; instead welcome it, and allow the experience to "ruin" your life by meeting head-on the misconceptions we discover about God, ourselves, and others.

Section II

Seven Convictions to Absorb

6

VISION

The engine that pulls the train

In my relatively brief time on this planet, I have observed that organizations budget in one of two ways:

1. THE TYPICAL WAY

The staff of many church and para-church groups show up to the annual planning meeting with this in mind: "Well, last year I was allotted this much for my ministry budget. If I jack it up about 10 percent and complain about all the shortages, maybe I'll walk away with at least a 5 percent increase." Or maybe their vision and thinking is limited by how much they think might come during the coming year: "Let's see, last year $746,000 came in. The economy is kind of down this year. Hey, if we received the same amount this year, how much ministry do you think we could accomplish?"

2. THE BILL BRIGHT WAY

I don't want to put anyone on a pedestal, but I have a tremendous amount of respect for Bill Bright, the late founder of Cru. My understanding is that he would gather his ministry directors from around the world for a planning session every year. Each director laid out to the others what he or she believed God wanted to do through their particular ministry the next 12 months. No one was allowed to mention how much different programs might cost until after they had prayed, discussed, and agreed on the overall Cru ministry plan for the upcoming year. Then, and only then, did they start attaching price tags. Afterward, Dr. Bright would draw a line under the total and say something like, "Here is what we believe God wants us to do throughout the world this next year. The total is $246 million. Now let's trust Him and go out and raise those funds to fulfill this vision."

Do you see the difference? Budget pulls one train, vision the other. One way is focused on what things cost, the other on how to fulfill the mission. Sometimes a person will ask me how much a certain project or equipment or materials or training costs, and I'll shoot back, "It doesn't matter, because we're going to spend whatever it takes to fulfill God's calling for our ministry." We are in an invisible, worldwide spiritual battle over the eternal destiny of billions of souls, and thus: **Strategicness always trumps thriftiness!**

John R. Mott, a Cornell college student in the 1880s who went on to ignite the Student Volunteer Movement and later win the 1946 Nobel Peace Prize as one of the greatest missionary statesman of all time, said: "Without a doubt, there comes to many of us the choice between a life of contraction or one of expansion; a life of small dimensions or one of widening horizons, larger visions and plans."

Budget or vision: Which one pulls your train?

7

PRAYER

Only God can turn hearts

"Prayer is the real work of the ministry. Service is just gathering in the results of prayer."

— S.D. Gordon in *Quiet Talks on Prayer*

The times in my life when I've applied this principle, I have seen God do some incredible things. Then why don't I employ this truth every day in every situation, you ask? I must have a short memory and a proud heart!

The amount of time I spend in prayer can indicate whether I am trusting in God or myself. Sometimes I foolishly think my presence with someone is more powerful and life-changing than God's presence. I can spend two hours with someone in a support appointment and thoroughly enjoy myself. But if you ask me to spend two minutes (a *whole* 120 seconds!) praying for them, it seems like an agonizing eternity.

Whatever else we do when support raising, we can't afford to neglect prayer. Here are three thoughts on making the most of what Gordon calls the "real work" of our ministry:

1. ACKNOWLEDGE THE POWER SOURCE

Psalm 62:11 tells us that "power belongs to God." So we better plug into the power source! As much as I'd like to reach down into someone's chest and turn his heart toward God (or toward me and our ministry), *only* God can do that. Whether it's witnessing or raising support, our persuasiveness and eloquence only goes so far. Isn't it preposterous that God has chosen to do His work in response to our prayers? For us to have the privilege of partnering with God to accomplish His work is the mother of all mismatches. Just don't forget who the managing partner is!

2. GO TO GOD FIRST

I just finished making a list of people I want to approach this month. I'm asking some to join our monthly team for the first time, others to re-start, and a few regular givers to consider increasing. My plan is all in place, except for one minor detail. I haven't "made my requests known to God" as commanded in Philippians 4:5-6. A Christian leader once said to me, "We must talk to God about men before we talk to men about God." The Lord will go before us and open doors and hearts — but He wants us to *ask* Him to do it!

3. MAKE SPECIFIC REQUESTS

The Bible teaches, "We have not because we ask not." I believe the Lord is waiting on us to *ask* Him. I once went through a list of about 20 people who've given us significant end-of-the-year gifts. I prayed for each person and asked God to lay a certain amount on that person's heart to give for that year. Yes, some years I go and ask certain people to invest the particular amount I prayed for, but sometimes I just ask God to put that amount in their hearts. I have enough answered prayers to fill a George Muller sequel! And when our specific requests are specifically answered, only He can get the credit.

NOTE: *Along with promptly thanking a donor who provides a special gift or increase, we shouldn't neglect to express appreciation to our Lord, the true source of the gift. Why? Because only God can turn hearts.*

8

SACRIFICE

Support raisers set the pace in giving

A group of missionaries from various agencies decided to meet each week for accountability. They resolved to be completely honest about their time with God, marriages, private lives, and finances. After about three months, the leader — I'll call him Rick — asked each person to share with the group what percentage of their income they were giving away. The answers shocked him:

- *"Income? I don't consider the support we've raised as income. I don't feel right about giving away funds that others have specifically sent for us."*

- *I think my time is more valuable than my money. We don't give much away at all, but we more than make up for it with the hours that we put in the ministry."*

- *"I don't know, maybe 2-3 percent each month. But I don't feel bad in light of the fact we're only at 78 percent of our support budget. We'll give more as our support increases."*

- *"We did a Bible study on debt and got convicted. So now all our funds are going to pay off debt. As soon as we're debt free, we will funnel that money to giving."*

The next week Rick prepared a handout for the group about why Christian workers should lead the way in giving. Here were his main points:

1. ALL BELIEVERS ARE COMMANDED TO GIVE

Rick listed 1 Corinthians 16:2, where Paul told the Corinthians to set aside funds "every week" to give and that it should be according to the level of their income. He also included Acts 20:35, where Jesus revealed a God-given, built-in instinct in all of us — that it is "more blessed to give than to receive." Noting these verses were for all Christians (even ones on support!), Rick posed a question to the group: "Will God continue to lead others to give to our ministries if we are not willing to obey Him in our own giving?"

yipes!

2. WE MUST MODEL WHAT WE ASK OTHERS TO DO

Rick mentioned how God modeled giving when He gave us His only Son (John 3:16) and how we dare not ask someone to sacrifice and give to us if we aren't first setting the pace. He challenged the group to follow the example of the Macedonian church, which was "rich in generosity" even though its members faced "extreme poverty" and "severe trials" (2 Corinthians 8:1-2). Then he asked: "Should our giving to God's work take an even higher priority than asking others to give to us and our work?"

3. WE REAP WHAT WE SOW

We can't fool God, Rick said, and He has created some basic cause-and-effect principles that apply to all people. He backed it up by quoting Proverbs 11:25 where "the generous man will be prosperous and he who waters will himself be watered." He challenged the group to come up with some specific action steps to begin giving sacrificially, consistently, joyfully, and secretly — and if they did, he said, God would reward them (Matthew 6:4). Rick left them with a final question: "Do we want to get to heaven and find out all our supporters have built up huge bank accounts, only to receive an 'insufficient funds' notice on our own meager accounts?"

NOTE: *For more on this topic, see Chapter 56.*

9

FULL FUNDING

The 100% imperative

Backbone. I know we all have one — it's just hard to find sometimes! Jesus was full of "grace and truth," but most of us choose grace over truth more than we'd like to admit. Even though exercising tough love with our staff (and ourselves) may inhibit some of the close emotional bonding we all yearn for, it's usually the right path to take.

All this to say: You are doing you and your co-workers a huge favor if not one single staff person is allowed to report to his ministry assignment without at least 100 percent of his monthly budget raised (not just pledged).

I know your organization may be anxious to launch new staff as quickly as possible, but cutting corners on this standard will come back to haunt you.

Most new staffers who beg to start early — while promising to keep working on support — never get to full budget. Why? Because if they are allowed to move to their ministry assignment, their support raising will go to the bottom of their "to-do" lists each week. The newness and excitement of their ministry will far outweigh the nagging need to make calls and have appointments. As a result, their ministry suffers, their marriage suffers, and the long-term stress will force many out of full-time service. So, if you're looking for short-term, marginally effective people who feel emotionally and spiritually drained, then turn a blind eye to this critical issue. Having financially healthy staff is not the key to ministry success, but it sure goes a long way toward creating good morale, happier marriages, staff retention, and new staff recruiting.

Am I sounding a little too dogmatic? I guess it's from years of listening to the horror stories of person after person, couple after couple in so many organizations. I remember one ministry where many of the single staff guys were at such low support they felt compelled to go give blood several times a week just to put food on the table. Needless to say, people were not lining up to join that staff!

Of course, having this policy and enforcing it are two different things. Get with the decision-makers in your organization and determine if you are willing to insert this standard into the mix. Then figure out how you will implement this policy and follow-through plan. You may not win a popularity contest the first few months, but in the long run your staff will rise up and bless you. Funny how others tend to respect us a little bit more when they see we really do have a backbone!

NOTE: *See Chapter 27 for suggestions on what to do when a veteran staffer's support dips below 100 percent.*

10

ASKING

A biblical approach to support raising

After college, I was in a self-sufficient "survival mode" stage of life where I dared not ask anyone for anything. My buddy and I lived in a $56-a-month ($28 each!) second-floor single room, sharing a bath with two other apartments. It was such low rent, we took a marker and wrote above one door the numeral "2," above the other door "2B," and above our door "Not 2B." Bringing visitors upstairs, I would point to the door numbers and proudly proclaim: "2B or Not 2B, that is the question!"

The question for Christian workers who raise their support is whether they should take the initiative to actually ask others to invest in them and their ministries. To ask or not to ask, that is the question. I am puzzled, though, why some Christian workers feel free to ask people to pray but not to give. Where in the Bible does it say "prayer good, giving bad"? If I went into an appointment, laid out my ministry vision, and "the ask" was just to pray and not to give, I would feel dishonest — even manipulative. Isn't it obvious to all parties the missionary needs support to go do his ministry?

In my decades of church involvement, I have heard many more sermons on giving than praying. Why would it be acceptable for churches to challenge us to give, but a "no-no" for missionaries to ask? Are we still living in the 1800s, continuing to exalt George Muller as our role model? He technically never asked for money, but instead spent the final decades of his life preaching every night to packed-out audiences all over the world, telling story after story — all with the same final point: "and I have never asked anyone for one single penny!" So much money was pouring in he had to give away huge surpluses! Lift up Muller as an ideal for faith, prayer, or preaching, but unless you have a worldwide pulpit ministry like his, you may not want to use him as your fund-raising model! Two passages that might help:

1. WE HAVE NOT BECAUSE WE ASK NOT (JAMES 4:2)

yikes!

Could it be that if we really got in touch with our motives we would find a basic fear of asking that has colored our theology and our approach? There's a reason the root word "ask" is found 147 times in the New Testament. God wants us to ask Him and others. Personally, I believe it takes more faith to pray and ask than simply to pray.

2. WHERE YOUR TREASURE IS, THERE IS YOUR HEART ALSO (MATTHEW 6:21)

You may have a different experience, but I've never had someone I sensed was praying for me who chose not to give to me. If they are willing to give to me, they are more likely to pray for me, too. This is why I don't have a support team and a separate prayer team. I have a support team of ministry partners whom I am trying to involve in intercession for me and my ministry. The principle of this passage is: If your donors begin to give, their hearts will start to engage, and they will grow to be the best prayer warriors you'll ever have!

Having emphasized the necessity and power of asking, I have (once in a blue moon) heard a small voice say, "Don't ask right now, just pray and love." Discerning whether that is God's voice or my fears is the secret!

NOTE: *We will address the concept of asking others for support throughout this book. My prayer is that you will see that particular approach as not only good, but biblical.*

TRAINING

Get the best, be the best

I won't bore you with the oh-so-familiar children's story of Goldilocks stumbling upon the three bears' house in the woods (with no one home) only to test their porridge, chairs, and beds. You remember — each time she tasted, sat, or laid down she would proclaim it be too little, too much, etc., and then, finally, "Juuuust right!"

Looks like I bored you anyway, but let's apply this tale to the critical area of support-raising training. Since the year 2000, we've been privileged to train staff from almost 500 organizations. You might ask, "So Steve, how many different approaches have you seen as groups seek to train their staff?" I would laugh and respond, "About 500!" Well, how much support training should a ministry provide? Most supply far too little training, some too much, and precious few ... "Juuuust right!" No, I don't believe one size fits all, but here are a couple of ministries that, in my opinion, have "figured it out."

Maybe we can learn from them:

CRU

In early 2000, I flew down to Daytona, Florida, to participate in Cru's Ministry Partner Development training. I joined 89 new staffers, all of us gladly trading $750 and six days of our lives for the intensive training provided by Ellis Goldstein and his nine full-time coaches. Morning, noon, and night we interacted with the Scriptures, prepared our presentation notebooks, and role-played until asking others to join our team became second nature. Did you pick up on how much emphasis this organization puts on training?

- They actually charge their staff $750-plus to make sure they really value it.
- They spend six full days doing nothing but support training.

- At least 10 full-timers focus exclusively on training and coaching staff.
- They even follow it up with regional trouble-shooting sessions each quarter.

THE NAVIGATORS

That fall, I trekked to Glen Eyrie, the Navigators' headquarters in Colorado Springs, Colorado, to soak in their support-raising training, as well. They charged $550 for the training and required that we invest at least 15 hours of Bible study before we came. The excellent training Scott Morton, Kevin DeFelice, and their team provided/ required included more Bible study, prayer, and even phoning real, live human beings, practicing asking for appointments. All new staffers had their direct supervisors sitting right next to them, going through the entire four days with them. The supervisor then had weekly accountability with them until 100 percent was reached.

Pick up any more tips?

- They could not come unless they spent at least 15 hours preparing.
- It moved from role-plays to actual calls.
- Afterward, it was not group, but one-on-one, weekly accountability.

Now, you're probably not part of a mega-organization like Cru or Navs where you can duplicate what I've described. But a crucial element of leadership is discerning what you can do excellently "in-house" and what you can't. If you don't have the expertise, personnel, or resources to do an A-plus job in the area of support raising training then you might consider partnering with some skilled specialists who can bring that piece of the puzzle to the table.

That may sound like a shameless commercial for our SRS Bootcamp training, but that's not my intent. Our single motive? To do whatever we can to help you and your organization get your new and veteran staff members to 100 percent of their funding and keep them there over the course of their life and ministry. Whether you provide that training yourself or choose to partner with an organization like ours, don't settle for too little (or even too much), but make sure it's "juuuust right!"

NOTE: *These organizations are just two of many that invest tremendous amounts of time and resources into their people in this area. InterVarsity, Chi Alpha, Mission Aviation Fellowship, Wycliffe — the list goes on!*

12

VALIDITY

Support raising is just as biblical as tentmaking

S upport raising and tentmaking are two biblical models for funding ministry, but sometimes they're pitted against one another.

Have you ever had someone respond to your support request by asking, "Why don't you go out and do your ministry the biblical way?" Curious, you inquire further, and they confidently proclaim, "Well, Jesus was a carpenter and Paul was a tentmaker. They didn't go and beg for support. They took care of themselves." While this is *a* descriptive way of doing ministry, I dare not push it as *the* prescriptive way for every Christian worker. To validate this approach, let's check out a couple of examples:

A LOOK AT JESUS

Even though Jesus could have impressed everyone with an endless supply of instant cash, He designed and implemented His plan to depend on God — and others — for support (Luke 8:1-3). If the Son of God funded his personal and ministry expenses from the ongoing support of individuals, why are we unwilling to embrace it, too? He also called 12 men to leave their jobs and follow Him, even training them on how to live and minister from the support of others (Luke 10:1-11). It's incredulous that some people are too proud to humble themselves to live and minister on support when that is exactly what God on earth did.

Bottom line: Jesus chose interdependence over independence.

A LOOK AT PAUL

I can only find three places in my New Testament where Paul made tents:

1. THESSALONICA (2 THESSALONIANS 3:8-9)

Even though Paul spent a very short period of time with this young church, he immediately recognized them as being lazy and even using their newfound doctrine on the second coming as an excuse not to work. Apparently they had read one too many *Left Behind* books and were waiting on the rooftops — instead of out building them! So Paul modeled what it meant to work hard during his short two-week stay there.

2. EPHESUS (ACTS 20: 33-34)

Paul's ministry there moved the converts to quit buying idols of the goddess Diana. If Paul had taken money from believers there, he might have been accused of putting the myriad of heathen craftsmen out of business for personal gain. He chose to forego support for a brief time in order to win the lost.

3. CORINTH (ACTS 18:4-5)

Paul was temporarily making tents — and thus only able to preach on Sabbaths — but when Silas and Timothy arrived (with financial support), he began devoting himself "exclusively to preaching." In 1 Corinthians 9, Paul zealously defends his right to be supported by the Corinthians, but because of their immaturity (including accusing Paul of preaching for profit), he briefly chose to support himself to be "above reproach."

Bottom line: Paul's preferred mode of operation? Full-time ministry!

A number of nations around the world don't take missionary visas, so a believer is required to work a secular job and legitimately contribute to the economy of the closed country. Even then, many of these "tentmakers" have support teams back home to fully fund their living and ministry expenses.

Like Paul, we shouldn't pit these two methods of support against each other. Instead, do whatever's needed to get the Gospel out. So next time someone attempts to shame you into working a secular job (instead of raising support for your ministry), just smile, pat them on the back, and move on, knowing you've done your homework — even if they haven't!

Section III

Eight Attitudes to Radiate

13

TEACHABILITY

Getting 'buy in' from your supporters

E mily was a 35-year-old teacher with quite a heart for missions. She had read various missionary biographies, gone on short-term mission trips, and prayed daily through Global Prayer Digest, but she felt a call to do more. After applying to several ministries, she arrived at a critical crossroads and began thinking seriously about accepting one of the staff opportunities presented to her.

She prayed, fasted, and read Scripture until she finally thought she knew God's will. Overjoyed, Emily immediately put together a newsletter list of 300-plus people to inform them of the good news. The headline read, "EMILY GOING TO CAMBODIA WITH FMO AGENCY" with a subtitle of "Read below how God led me to my decision." She was confident she would instantly be inundated with calls, emails, congratulations, even checks. But it was not to be. Other than the message she got from her stunned father, almost no one seemed to acknowledge this momentous declaration. Discouragement set in, and she was already questioning her newfound "calling."

Where did Emily go wrong? Was she a terribly unloved person or was her church just not missions-minded enough? Neither! Emily simply forgot a fundamental principle of human nature, one she'd used a thousand times in her classroom: If you want others to "*buy in*" you better first let them "*weigh in!*"

Whether you're asking fifth-graders which of three books they prefer reading or asking 300 potential donors their opinions of which career path you should pursue, you can almost never go wrong by inquiring, "What do you think?" So if you're considering embarking on a new ministry (or a transition to a new position or organization) and you want to have (or maintain) a strong support team, you might want to read and heed the following:

1. ALWAYS HONOR AND INCLUDE YOUR SUPPORTERS

Instead of just announcing to everyone that God has spoken to you and now you are delivering that pronouncement to the masses, why not take a more humble, teachable approach? Whether you're just getting started or a ministry veteran, showing respect and dignity toward your supporters will produce interest and appreciation (and support!) in your life and ministry.

2. WITH MANY COUNSELORS THERE IS VICTORY (PROVERBS 15:22)

You'll be amazed when you apply this passage and seek the advice and input of the people in your world. Asking is normally better received than telling, and besides, you never know how the Lord may speak through your family, spiritual leaders, friends, and, yes, even your potential financial supporters. Some of them might know you better than you know yourself, offering some keen insight. They love you and want what's best for your life. Don't shut them out!

3. THE GREATER THE INVESTMENT, THE GREATER DESIRE FOR INPUT

Segment your contacts into three groups:

- Who are the 6-10 people who might be able and willing to be *major* prayer and financial stakeholders in your ministry? Go to them personally to ask them to pray and think *with* you, to give you feedback and questions.

- Identify 8-12 potential *medium* stakeholders and (at least) phone them for their advice.

- Finally, send out a mass newsletter to everyone, sharing your heart and journey in life and ministry, including all your contact info, and asking for their counsel or concerns.

And when it comes time for you to ask for support, these three groups will feel greater ownership and loyalty to you. They will much more likely "*buy* in" because you gave them a chance to "*weigh* in!"

NOTE: *For a case study on how this attitude and approach has been applied, see Chapter 49.*

14

PATIENCE

Why shortcuts only short-circuit!

Before the days of Mapquest and GPS, I remember a particularly important road trip where I began poring over a map and predicting I could shave 50 miles and 60 minutes off our travel time. Projecting supreme confidence, I exited the interstate to "cut the corner," anticipating speeding along a lonely country road and getting to our destination in record time. But, after spending two long hours crawling through dinky little towns, getting stuck behind hay trailers, and wearing out a set of brakes on a myriad of hairpin turns, I finally had to admit to my now frustrated passengers that I was a total idiot and we were going to be an hour late rather than an hour early!

Why is it we seem to *always* seek the easiest, quickest, and least painful way to accomplish something? Maybe you, like me, rejected your mom's old-fashioned warning of "haste makes waste," stubbornly insisting your way would be better and faster. Don't feel alone; from Henry Ford mass-producing Model Ts to the "get rich quick" tech stock day-traders of the 1990s, we Americans want it and we want it now! Sadly, many Christian workers have been lured into this thinking, too. Instead of paying the price in time, money, and effort to diligently establish a deep, solid, long-term support team that will last a lifetime, they desperately look for shortcuts. They may turn out to be "cheap substitutes" that initially look good on the outside, but may very well bring disappointment down the road. Here are three examples:

1. BANQUETS

Everyone loves a good meal, a speaker, and a slide show. We've all experienced the heart-tugging appeal, the filling out of the commitment card, and the gregarious emcee shouting the grand total raised. These are fun and can increase awareness, but some organizations spend more time planning funding events (banquets, golf tourneys, auctions, etc.) than fulfilling the witnessing and discipling goals of their ministry! I can promise you that twenty hours planning a big bash won't produce a fraction of the results of twenty one-hour support appointments. And many of the people who write the obligatory $75 "one-time" checks at banquets would commit to investing $100 to $150 *per month* if someone took the time to meet with and ask them individually.

2. CHURCH TOURS

Some Christian workers pack up their family and presentation materials and go from town to town, church to church sharing about their ministry and needs. Their theory is that if they can just preach enough rousing sermons, apply to enough mission committees, or get enough folks to sign their newsletter list, then full support is right around the corner — all the while frantically praying the "love offerings" somehow cover all the fast food, cheap hotels, and gasoline bills! But instead of producing strong monthly support teams, these (6-, 12-, 18-month) ill-advised "vision trips" usually result in nothing more than worn-out kids, disillusioned spouses, and broken-down cars.

3. PLEDGE CARDS

Many Christian workers mail or hand pledge cards to donors, but I cannot, for the life of me, figure out why. I'm not trying to be critical, but what is the *real* motive in mailing/giving someone a pledge card? Some say they act as a "silent reminder" continuing to make "the ask" on our behalf. But if your mode of operation each time is to:

- *Meet* with them face to face
- *Invite* them to come on your team
- *Call* them back (if need be) for a decision
- *Come by* to pick up the first check

Please tell me what a pledge card does for you?

Conclusion: I don't mind you (or them) filling out an "Information Card" so you'll have their phone, address, email, etc., and some think there's value in having them sign a card expressing their commitment. Yes, I can see how both of these ideas might be of help, but here's my admonition: Don't ever do *anything* that substitutes for the personal, one-on-one approach. Please don't let anyone talk you into building your support-raising strategy around fancy banquets, whirlwind church tours, or colorful pledge cards. More times than not these *shortcuts* will only *short-circuit* your support-raising plans! Think for a moment: How would *you* want to be approached and treated? Here's a rule to go by: Do unto others as you would have them do unto you.

The Golden Rule!

15

COURAGE

Walk toward your fears

After helping train thousands of staff members from a host of Christian ministries, I have come to a conclusion: Ministries do personal support raising just like they do their personal witnessing. Consider the necessary steps in both activities:

1. Create the need
2. Share the solution
3. Ask for a decision

Even though rejection is possible, the bottom line for both endeavors is: Are you able to ask the "golden question?"

After presenting the Gospel to someone, the golden question is sometimes the most agonizingly difficult question in the English language. Even typing it out, my hands are sweating, my heart is pounding, and my throat is dry. Posing the question, "Would you like to receive Jesus Christ into your life as your Lord and Savior right now?" and then locking my eyes onto theirs, zipping up my lips and waiting for their response is harder to do than swallowing rancid pig intestines on reality TV. They might say "no" and I hate to be rejected, so I let this "fear factor" shape my theology by rationalizing away the need to ask people to receive Christ, claiming God is surely big enough to save someone without my puny little questions.

The fears we face in evangelism are the exact ones we experience in support raising. As a result, many Christian workers will only use desserts, appeal letters, pledge cards, etc., to do their asking for them. And even those who actually meet with donors one-on-one sometimes can't bring themselves to mouth the words of the infamous support-raising golden question: "Mr. Smith, it would be such an honor to have you and your family investing in us and our ministry.

I am wondering if you would consider supporting us for $100 or even $150 a month? What do you think?" Once again, zip the lip and let them answer. It is now *their* turn to talk!

Again, why do many Christian workers choose not to ask? Deep down it is basically a fear of rejection.

I don't get my jollies out of making people feel uncomfortable, so I ask my golden questions as casually and as relationally as possible — but I still ask. Think about it. As a Christian worker (who is being supported by others to supposedly fulfill the Great Commission), if I can't even ask the simple golden question in evangelism, how am I ever going to be able to ask it in support raising? Furthermore, do I even have the right to?

If you or your staff are struggling mustering up the courage to ask people face-to-face to join your personal support teams, you might evaluate how you're doing in the area of asking others to believe and receive Christ into their lives. If you can break through the faith barriers in witnessing, it will shoot adrenaline into your soul, giving you the courage to walk toward your fears in support raising.

Hint: Once you've asked enough people the golden question in your witnessing, asking others the question in support raising is no big deal!

16

AFFIRMATION

Asking big esteems supporters

There I was, mesmerized by the vision and passion of this campus staff worker who was pouring out his heart to reach the world for Christ and asking me to join his support team. But when the moment of truth arrived and he shared how much he was asking me to invest, I could not believe it. He only asked me for $35 a month! I was stunned and embarrassed for him. Was that *all* his vision was worth? Was that *all* he thought I could (or would) give? Guess how much I agreed to contribute? Yep, just $35 a month. We think we offend people by asking too *high*, but with most people, we offend them by asking too *low*!

About a year later, I was approached by two different men who presented their ministry to me — but with just an average degree of vision and passion. When the time came to ask me to join their team, they each asked me for $200 a month. Guess how much I agreed to give each of their teams? Yep, $35 a month. I guess I was stuck on that figure, but I will never forget the courage they displayed and the dignity they showed me (and themselves). Instead of being offended, I was honored because they not only believed I was *generous* enough to give that much, but that I also had the *ability* to. They thought I was willing *and* able. I would have liked to meet their expectation, and if they do a good job connecting with me over the years, I might just gradually increase to that figure someday.

A great story to illustrate this principle is from the life of Napoleon, the famous general (and later emperor) of France. After a particularly long and brutal battle, Napoleon and his army finally conquered a highly prized Mediterranean island and its many inhabitants. Afterward, while he and his generals were sitting, drinking, and savoring the victory, a young officer approached

Napoleon. When the revered general asked the man what he wanted, he looked straight at Napoleon and said, "Sir, give me this island." All the other generals began to laugh and mock the presumptuous young man, that is until Napoleon turned and asked one of them for a pen and another for paper. To their amazement, Napoleon wrote out a deed to the island, signed it, and handed it to the bold, but lowly soldier.

"How could you do that?" stammered one of his generals, "What made this man worthy to receive this great island after we fought so hard to win it?"

"I gave him this island," Napoleon replied, "because he honored me by the magnitude of his request."

Are you or any of your fellow staff afraid of asking for too much? You can always come down into a more comfortable range for the donor. But how much are you and your ministry worth? $100, $200, $300 or more a month? Ask big. You won't offend them. In fact, you'll probably affirm and honor them by the magnitude of your request. My former pastor, Dr. H.D. McCarty says, "When I get to heaven, I don't want to be guilty of asking God — or others — for too little." Me neither.

NOTE: *For examples and principles of "asking big," see Chapter 50.*

17

CONFIDENCE

Big visions require big dollars

Years ago a friend of mine worked for a prominent businessman who invited him along for an appointment with Bill Bright, then the president of Cru. In that meeting, Dr. Bright asked this businessman for $1 million dollars to help fund worldwide evangelism projects. My friend knew the businessman didn't have the funds, but still he committed to the requested amount. Later I learned there were almost 250 other individuals who also committed at least $1 million. Cru dubbed this group of sacrificial investors, "History's Handful."

My intention isn't to keep exalting Bill Bright, but he has been a pioneer and pacesetter for all of us in so many ways. How do you explain the hundreds (even thousands) of people around the world who committed huge amounts of money to him and the Great Commission plans he presented to them? All I can think of is: *Big Visions Require (and Attract!) Big Dollars*. Dr. Bright's vision was so big, so compelling, so "God-sized" that myriads of givers wanted to join him and get a "fraction of the action."

Nehemiah, who lived almost 2,500 years ago, was another man who dared to dream big and who even risked his life to ask wealthy, powerful people to put up the venture capital to make those dreams a reality. Here are a few simple principles He lived by:

1. NEHEMIAH *PRAYED* BIG

Most of Nehemiah Chapter 1 presents his response to the news that his beloved Jerusalem had fallen into physical and spiritual ruin. He was so burdened that all he could do was mourn and weep — and pray. After confessing sins on behalf of *all* the Jews, he claimed the promise the Lord made to Moses to re-gather His people to Israel

(Nehemiah 1:8,9). Against all odds, this cupbearer exiled in a far away land believed God for the impossible.

2. NEHEMIAH *PLANNED* BIG

He prayed in faith but did not stop there. He got up off his knees and started to strategize. He knew this was a God-sized project that required God-sized resources. So, after specifically asking the Lord for an open door with King Artaxerxes (1:11), Nehemiah mapped out his plans and presentation so as not to give any nebulous answers during his support appointment with the King. I don't know whether or not Nehemiah majored in engineering in college, but he did an excellent job putting all the details together of what kind of time, materials, and manpower it would take to finish the job.

3. NEHEMIAH *ASKED* BIG

When Artaxerxes quizzed him about what he wanted, Nehemiah didn't stutter, but passionately asked, "Send me to Judah, to the city of my fathers' tombs, that I may rebuild it." (Nehemiah 2:5) After painting the big picture for the king, he followed with more detailed requests for letters of introduction and building materials. He knew what the king was capable of and he wanted to make sure his ask was commensurate with the giver's abilities. (You don't ask someone who can fund your whole project for $100 a month!) As the king listened to the huge vision brewing within Nehemiah's heart, this humble but courageous servant didn't back down. Instead, he proceeded to ask for a God-sized gift. Why? He knew that only big visions draw big dollars.

18

RESTORATION

Old friends can become new supporters

Back in the day, my old friend Stevie and I made an unbeatable tandem in fourth-grade YMCA football — one would block, while the other would carry the ball. I have such fond memories of Stevie and all the touchdowns we teamed up on. The only problem is, I haven't talked to him in more than 40 years!

Now, what if I were launching out on a personal fundraising tour and some crazy support-raising trainer told me to write down "every person I have ever known in my life" on my name-storming list? And then he challenges me to go back and try to re-connect with old friends like Stevie, asking them to come onto my monthly support team. What would I think of this idea, you ask?

I would think he had totally lost his mind!

I have to believe that the precise moment I call and Stevie picks up the phone and I start into my "let's catch up" talk, he will suspect I want something — probably to sell him insurance! This fear is real, but it doesn't have to keep us from re-connecting with friends from 5, 10, 20, 30, yes even 40 years ago. I bet if you really brainstormed you could come up with a thousand people you've met during your lifetime. I doubt you are keeping up with a hundred of them. If you try to re-connect with the other 900 and they say "no thanks," what have you lost? Nothing!

Here's how to get started:

- Look up the addresses and phone numbers of every elementary, junior high, senior high, and college friend you've ever had. Then search Facebook to add as many as possible to your friend list.

- Compose a "pre-call" letter to each. After writing a personalized greeting and intro paragraph, briefly catch them up on your growing up years, conversion to Christ, family, job, and how God has now led you into ministry.

Some thoughts I would include somewhere in my "pre-call" letter:

> *As you can tell, Steve, my life has changed and I'm excited, but nervous, about my calling into college ministry. I feel like Evel Knievel peering over the Grand Canyon, about to attempt a jump with my motorcycle! There will be 4,500 freshmen invading our campus August 15, and I want to be there to befriend them and lead them to Christ. This is the greatest challenge I've ever faced, and I'm trusting God, but I also realized … I need help!*
>
> *My organization requires me to raise all of my personal and operational expenses before I can launch my ministry, and so I've been praying and thinking of key individuals who have had a part in my life over the years. So at this critical juncture I'm going back to the very roots of my life and asking old friends like you to allow me to share with them the ministry vision and financial goals the Lord has laid before me.*
>
> *Steve, I know it's been decades since we have seen each other, but at one time in our lives you meant something to me and I meant something to you. You may or may not be willing or able to join me and invest in this new venture, but it would be an honor to share my story with you — and to catch up after all these years! I would like to give you a call next week and see if there might be a time to meet. I look forward to re-connecting.*

Now, is that so scary? Sure, they might say no. But what could happen? An old friend just might become a new supporter!

NOTE: *To read an account of how someone used this approach, see Chapter 52.*

19

HONOR

Face-to-face asking is the most personal

If you are engaged or married (or think you someday will be), this survey is for you.

Question: What was the method used in initiating the marriage commitment with your partner? Was the proposal made through:

1. A letter
2. A phone call
3. A fax
4. Email
5. Text message
6. Facebook
7. Face to face

I've given this "Marriage Proposal Method Survey" to hundreds of people and, almost without exception, No. 7 was the resounding response. Amazing! Even in our age of technology, the old fashion personal approach was deemed best. Apparently, even though we've become high-tech, we still need to be high-touch. In fact, some of the wives I surveyed said, "I wouldn't have married him unless he looked right into my eyes and asked me." Occasionally, I then turned to the husband and asked him where he got the idea, the words, the courage to propose to his wife face to face.

This whole survey is a farce, isn't it? Of course the proposal is made face to face because it is a very, very important ask. Now, "Will you support me?" is not quite as critical as "Will you marry me?" but the principle is this: "If it's important, we will do it face to face."

Whether it's a marriage proposal, a late-night session with your teenager, or having to fire someone at work, if it's important, it needs to be done face to face. So, why do we take shortcuts and substitute in a letter, a call, a banquet, or a pledge card to do the asking for us? Not sure, but it's no wonder the potential supporter doesn't feel honored and consequently doesn't join our team. Not only do they think you don't care about them, but what you're doing and what you're asking for must not be very important, either — otherwise you would have done it face to face!

The apostle John felt strongly about this concept: *"I have much to write to you, but I do not want to use paper and ink. Instead, I hope to visit you and talk with you face to face ..."* (2 John 1:12, NIV)

Know this for sure: How we go about asking people to join our team will determine what kind of supporters they'll be. If we choose the quick and easy route of a letter or call, they may come on our team, but many times it will be a shallow, short-term commitment for a smaller amount on an inconsistent basis. But if you will commit to the personalized and customized approach (like a marriage proposal), that person will always remember the respect, sensitivity, courage, and care you showed. Many will not be able to pull their checkbooks out fast enough in order to commit larger amounts — and for the long haul. There's something about a face-to-face encounter (including a verbal commitment) with someone that helps create an "expectations exchange" that will never be forgotten.

I have been on support since 1986 and almost everyone I met with face to face back then is still on my monthly team, still giving like clockwork, and even increasing every few years. You see, I'm not just looking for supporters. I want supporters *for life*! Like proposing, *how* you ask someone can make all the difference! Please, honor them by doing it face to face.

20

SELF RESPECT

'Poor talk' poisons you and your ministry

Question: What do college students standing in line at the dining hall have in common with a group of Christian ministry staffers gathered around the water cooler?

Answer: They're all complaining — one group about the food and the other about finances.

Many Christian ministries are infested with people who constantly whine about how much things cost, what they don't have, or how tight their budget is. They're drowning in an ocean of discontent and don't even realize it.

This pity party called "poor talk" usually surfaces in one of three ways:

- Joking ("The next time my husband takes me out to dinner will probably be at the marriage feast of the lamb in heaven!")
- Hinting ("We're hoping to get the air conditioner repaired when our support increases.")
- Comparing ("Sure would be nice to send our kids to a Christian school like the Newtons do.")

I giggle when I hear poor-talkers respond to compliments with their brand of disclaimers. They feel compelled to tell us their new shirt was on sale, their new camera was bought with tax refunds, and their vacation was paid for by an Internet coupon!

And instead of using our ministry newsletters to communicate vision and changed lives, we're tempted to manipulate the sympathies of our donors by sneaking poor talk into the "Prayer Request" section (e.g. "Pray that God would provide for our kids' dental needs. Pray someone would give us a computer. Pray our mission funds come in by December 1.")

This "poor me" attitude robs us of our self-respect, the dignity of our position and casts us as beggars in our supporters' eyes. Instead of just going out and inviting others (face to face) to invest in us and in our ministries, we rationalize, blame our circumstances, and slip into denial. This is usually when the credit cards come out! Other toxic consequences include:

1. POOR TALK POISONS MINISTRY MORALE

When people are more focused on saving pennies at the grocery store than they are winning the world to Christ, they have lost sight of the vision. Focusing on what we *don't* have rather than on the gifts and calling God has graciously provided is downright depressing!

2. POOR TALK POISONS OUR VIEW OF SPIRITUALITY

The opposite ditch from the health and wealth Gospel is the "being poor is more spiritual" perspective. This kind of theology is why some Christian workers are still driving that broken down '69 Subaru — and bragging about it.

3. POOR TALK POISONS STAFF RECRUITMENT

The fastest way to drive off potential staff candidates is for them to get a small (yet lethal) dose of poor talk from you or your co-workers. Most people want to join a staff that is strong spiritually, socially, emotionally, and financially.

There are stresses and pressures that come with living on support, but the solution is to set a healthy budget and then raise 100 percent of the funds in order to fully support your family and win this spiritual battle we are engaged in. And in the process: Do away with all poor talk!

NOTE: *For more on this topic, see Chapter 51.*

Section IV

Eight Questions to Ask

21

GOD OR OTHERS

Which should we ask for support?

Y ou really have to answer this question for yourself. To be of some help, let me give you a little history lesson about three men who answered this question in different ways. You may or may not have heard of these three godly saints from the past, but they have profoundly influenced us in this area of how a person should go about raising funds.

To begin with, you can tell a lot about an organization by when it was founded. Many of the older ones will use George Muller or Hudson Taylor (both from England) or America's D.L. Moody as a role model for fundraising.

Muller, a former lawyer turned prolific preacher, began numerous orphanages in London and trusted God alone for finances, claiming he never asked anyone for a single schilling. He spent the final 40 years of his life telling that story every night to overflow crowds in cities all over the world.

Taylor, a young missionary who struck out on his own, began the influential China Inland Mission Society in 1865. Reading his prayer journals is a lesson on faith and reveals that much of his financing actually came from excess donations that Muller passed on to him.

Moody, a barely educated mountain of a man, went from selling shoes in Boston to become the world's leading evangelist. He wrote and personally asked scores of people to invest big dollars in the Kingdom. He was criticized for being too brazen, but he kept on asking.

Here were their three philosophies of fundraising:

- Muller only prayed (No information, no solicitation)
- Taylor prayed and shared needs (Full information, no solicitation)
- Moody prayed, shared needs, and asked (Full information, full solicitation)

For me — and this is just me — it takes more faith to pray, make my needs known, and then ask someone face to face to invest in me and my ministry. The reason that I (and this is just me) would choose *not* to ask is pure and simple — fear. I could spiritualize it all I wanted, but I would be allowing fear of rejection to control me. For almost three decades now, by God's grace, I have been trying to walk toward my fears, not away from them.

I believe asking is a good thing. The words "ask" and "asking" are used all throughout the Old and New Testaments and obviously are a very common theme throughout.

I love and respect all three of these men, and I have read multiple biographies of each. You need to listen to the Lord to know what direction is right for you, but can you tell which of the three support-raising approaches I usually recommend to others? I'm sure you can! Later in life, Moody humorously penned a new beatitude: "Blessed are the money raisers, for in heaven they shall stand next to the martyrs." I'll see you there!

NOTE: *Ask God which of these approaches is the best for you. Don't let fear make your decision for you. "God has not given us a spirit of fear, but of love, power, and self control." (2 Timothy 1:7). And the question remains. Who should we ask for support — God or people? My answer of course, is BOTH!*

22

FULL-TIME OR PART-TIME:

Which support raising approach is best?

The arena was pitch black except for the spotlight on the man performing amazing feats 100 feet above the crowd. We would gasp as he'd let go of one trapeze, do multiple flips, then blindly fly toward a second trapeze he *believed* would be there. At the last split second, he'd grab the swinging metal bar and make it safely back to the platform. To any rational human being, this high-flying spectacle appears as pure lunacy.

In the same way, newly accepted Christian workers who deliberately walk away from their safe and secure regular paycheck in order to raise support full-time (without any visible means to pay the bills) are viewed as foolish (even fanatical) by many co-workers, family, even spiritual leaders. Such workers feel called to ministry, but they are torn between two worlds, not wanting to let go of one source of funds before they see the other definitely coming.

As a result, the support efforts of most new staff recruits consist of trying to squeeze in a few appointments each week around their work schedule. This plan may appear to be the most "sensible," but it has drawbacks:

1. TIME TO RAISE FULL SUPPORT CAN BE DOUBLED OR TROUBLED

A full-time support raiser can schedule 20-30 appointments weekly, but someone who continues to devote the best 40-50 hours of his week to a secular job will not have the time or energy to make and keep even one-third that many of face-to-face appeals. A six-month full-time effort can easily drag out to 18 or even 24 months of part-time focus.

2. NO ONE HAS A SENSE OF URGENCY

Donors hesitate to come on a team until the newcomer really needs support. Why? Givers want to invest in ministry, not just in support-raising efforts or swelling someone's ministry/savings account for some unknown beginning date in the future. Few feel passionately compelled to join a team unless they sense they're supporting a man or woman "on a mission," working diligently toward a goal.

A Case Study: Eric reached a crossroads in his life. The successful businessman with a growing family attended one of the BodyBuilders Ministry's *NVision* world mission seminars and he found himself deeply impacted. He began to wrestle with the Lord whether or not He was calling Eric into missions. He discussed it with his wife and pastor and began exploring opportunities with various agencies. He studied mission websites, talked with representatives from different ministries, and felt drawn to apply to several organizations. One small detail in the fine print held him back — almost all of them required that he *raise his own support.*

That one line struck fear in his heart because he knew full well he would need to raise a boatload of money just to cover the basic expenses he and his family accrued each month. Tempted to turn and quietly walk away from his sense of calling, he pressed ahead. His parents and business associates thought he'd lost his mind. His wife and kids were supportive, but asked numerous questions, as did he. How could he continue to work his normal 50-plus hours a week *and* raise support at the same time? He was sure people would wait to start supporting them until he actually left his job and salary, started the ministry, and *really* needed the funds.

An idea started to percolate in his mind. Eric and his wife called six couples — all close friends who had the resources to get behind him and his family. They all gathered one night in Eric's living room for coffee, dessert, and a "take the plunge" announcement. Eric started by sharing his testimony, his calling into missions, and the proposed ministry assignment. Then he leaned forward, looked around, and passionately spoke from his heart:

"We asked you here tonight to share with you the biggest step of faith we've ever taken. We want to get to our ministry quickly because multitudes are dying each day without Christ. But we cannot move to our ministry assignment and begin to reach them until we're at 100 percent of our support. I can't work 50 to 60 hours a week and have an appointment here and there on an evening or weekend. We will never make it! I need a five- to

six-month window of time where I can focus exclusively on packing out my mornings, noons, and nights with appointments. Yes, we're going to come to each of you to ask you to invest in us on a monthly basis, but tonight I'm asking you to consider taking a step of faith and sacrifice with us. Would you each write an upfront 2K, 4K, 6K, even $8,000 check in order to 'buy us' the time to raise our support? That way I can quit my job, still cover our bills, and dedicate the kind of time and money required to build a healthy, long-term support team. Will you pray about it and let me get back to each of you this week to see how the Lord has led you on this?"

One fascinating example of this from Scripture is Nehemiah (the highly motivated support raiser and construction engineer) who left his job with King Artaxerxes in order to focus full-time on gathering his resources and completing the task of rebuilding the wall. You may know that he pulled it all off in a mere 52 days! His secret? He was able to work on it FULL-TIME.

NOTE: *For a look at a successful businessman who took Eric's advice and met with tremendous receptivity and success, see Chapter 53.*

23

CHURCHES OR INDIVIDUALS

Which should you focus on?

I n March 2003, sportswriters for *USA Today* took a vote on the most difficult thing to do in all of sports and ranked hitting a 100 mph fastball as the toughest of all. Any major leaguer would concur, knowing it requires laser-like focus to connect with the tiny blur hurling toward you.

Similarly, a successful support raiser must exercise incredible concentration to get to a ministry assignment quickly and fully funded. In Bill Dillon's book, *People Raising*, he contrasts two different, but true, cases of support raising — one focused on churches, the other on individuals:

CASE ONE: COUPLE FOCUSED ON *CHURCHES*

- Support-raising training: None
- Raised support full-time
- Churches contacted: 164 (called, info packets sent)
- Church meetings: 51
- Number of supporting churches: 16
- Miles driven: 33,000
- Travel expenses: $8,530
- Time to get to 100 percent: 13 months

CASE TWO: SINGLE GIRL FOCUSED ON *INDIVIDUALS*

- Support-raising training: 1 day
- Raised support part-time (had 40 hour per week job)
- 106 initial letters sent to individuals
- 41 people called for appointments
- 38 appointments
- 31 pledged support
- 14 others called her to pledge, from word of mouth
- Time to get to 100 percent: 10 weeks

I know this is just two cases, but I have seen this played out many times. I believe you should ask your home church to anchor your support team for at least 20 percent of your total, and, if you have time, approach a few other key churches. But, in my opinion, if possible, the main focus of your support raising should be with individuals. Some denominations like their missionaries to go from church to church to raise support because it builds vision in those congregations (and I understand their reasoning), *but* the wear and tear on that traveling missionary can be substantial.

interesting

Here's the principle: Going to *people* you *do* know will almost always bear more fruit than going to *churches* you *don't* know. Here's why:

1. THE CHURCH APPROACH USUALLY TAKES LONGER

Even if you find churches that will meet with you, it takes time to work through the maze of church committees, policies, applications, and decision-making processes.

2. INDIVIDUALS ARE MORE PERSONAL

If a church comes on your team, there usually isn't one person with the specific responsibility of tracking with you. You want to have a personal, involved team of people to support you, not just organizations who send a check.

3. CHURCH LEADERS COME AND GO

I've been a pastor and elder in local churches. Turnover seems like a constant for many churches, and if a new pastor or missions committee chairman comes in that doesn't know you, your support may be at risk.

4. CHURCH SUPPORT USUALLY GOES TO THEIR OWN

The last 15 years, churches have been funneling more and more of their mission dollars toward launching their own members into ministry rather than doling out money to the revolving door of missionaries constantly passing through. I think there is wisdom to this, but it does wreak havoc on the missionaries who think "paper bombing" requests to hundreds of churches is the key to success.

Churches or individuals: Which will you focus on? Choose wisely and keep your eye on the ball.

24

A WORKING SPOUSE

Does it affect support raising?

Scenario 1: Reggie is a 25-year-old dynamo who was accepted onto the staff of an agency reaching out to Muslims. He received support-raising training and started working on it full-time. But four months into his efforts, he hit a wall. Person after person seemed hesitant to come on his team. When he probed a little deeper, some of his contacts responded, "Now, isn't your wife a CPA for the big accounting firm downtown?" How is Reggie to respond?

Scenario 2: Sarah is an energetic 32-year-old who, after getting married and nurturing two kids up to elementary age, wanted to go on staff with a local ministry reaching out to teenagers. To do so, they required her to raise $3,000 a month of support. She felt a little embarrassed, though, to ask friends and family for support, knowing her husband made well over $10,000 a month in his sales job. What should Sarah do?

Contrary to some spiritual leaders, I believe both men and women are equally qualified to do full-time ministry — as well as raising full support for that ministry. The Bible does touch on the different ministry functions God designed for men and women, but let's leave the male/female ministry role controversies for another day. Now we are just trying to help Reggie and Sarah, knowing that raising support when your spouse is working sometimes presents a dilemma involving biblical, cultural, and economic factors. This is a hot topic with a myriad of opinions, but if staff within your organization fit this category, here a couple of tips to keep in mind:

1. SOME POTENTIAL DONORS MIGHT BE HESITANT TO GIVE

If they know the support raiser has a spouse with a good job and salary, they will probably not say anything, but inwardly smile and think, "Hey, kinda' double dippin', huh?!" Their unwillingness to respond might conceal their doubts as to whether there is a real need to raise another full salary when the family already has a significant income.

2. THE STAFFER MIGHT NOT BE AS MOTIVATED

I've noticed over the years that a person will usually only raise what he *has* to raise. If he knows he can count on his spouse's $40,000-a-year coming in whether he raises 100 percent support or not, it's difficult to kindle a sense of urgency. This can produce a range of emotions, from embarrassment to guilt about asking others for support when it might *appear* there is not a legitimate need.

Also, some donors like to get "two for the price of one" and prefer that both husband and wife spend their work hours in the same ministry. This might be the ideal (and can aid the support-raising process), but it's not necessarily the norm. My hope is that you have support policies that fit your organization *and* people, taking into account the inherent challenges that exist when a support raiser has a spouse with an outside job and salary.

25

STANDARD OF LIVING

What should it be for Christian workers?

Fresh out of seminary, I found myself encircled by a distinguished board of successful doctors, lawyers, and businessmen quizzing me about my expectations for my starting salary as a new staff member at their church. Taking the "spiritual" route, I said I wasn't there for the money — so they ended up paying me only 60 percent of what my contemporaries were making! Looking back, I should have said, "I'm not here for the money. Just pay me a moderate salary. Why don't we just take the average of everyone's salary on this committee and pay me that? Not a penny more." I would have given a year's salary just to see the looks on their faces!

How much should a Christian worker make, and what should our standard of living be? The unwritten rules of the game seem to say it's OK for church staffers (especially of larger churches) to live at a higher level than missionaries who live on support. Deep down, many believers view support raising as begging, and, of course, beggars should barely get by. I wish I knew who made up these double standards!

Meanwhile, author Randy Alcorn claims we're *all* rich: "If you have sufficient food, decent clothes, live in a house that keeps the weather out, and own a reasonably reliable means of transportation, you are among the top 15 percent of the world's wealthy. If you have any money saved, a hobby that requires some equipment or supplies, a variety of clothes in your closet, two cars (in any condition), and live in your own home, you're in the top 5 percent." So, really, what we're talking about here is whether our staff will be in the top 3, 4, or 5 percent of the world's wealthy, right?

In approaching this delicate topic, I seek to abide by two seemingly competing principles:

1. LIVE A SPARTAN LIFESTYLE

This wartime way-of-life I'm describing here is unencumbered with the non-essentials and is, according to Pastor John Piper, a "glad hearted austerity that will make any sacrifice for the joy of being on the cutting edge of God's Kingdom." Jesus stripped Himself for spiritual battle — so should we. The more we acquire and surround ourselves with luxuries and toys, the more time and energy (read: distraction) are required. Finally, making lots of money is not the same as amassing wealth. John Wesley said, make as much as you can and give as much as you can.

2. MAXIMIZE YOUR FRUITFULNESS

Scott Morton, vice president of development for The Navigators, was asked how much support a Christian worker should raise. He said, "Raise enough to maximize the fruitfulness of your family and ministry."

He's not advocating a health and wealth theology, but neither is this a "poverty = spirituality" mindset. To "maximize fruitfulness" will be different for everyone. It may mean:

- Sending kids to a private school or taking an annual vacation together to help maximize the fruitfulness of your family

- Purchasing a high-powered computer or earning an additional degree in order to be the best steward you can with the ministry God has entrusted you with.

With all decisions, though, we must be careful not to judge others by *our* personal choices. So, should you drive a '69 Subaru or a brand new Lexus? Probably neither, but let God — not the expectations or standards of others — help you decide.

26

ASKING NON-BELIEVERS FOR SUPPORT

Is it wrong?

K ent came to Christ in college and instantly started growing. It wasn't long until he wanted to join a summer missions team to India. The only problem? He was required to raise $3,500 and he didn't have a home church, Christian family, or Christian friends. The only people he knew were his fraternity brothers. Sometimes Greek chapters do service projects to earn money to give to charitable causes, and so Kent asked his group if they would donate those funds to his mission trip. They agreed, as did two other houses he asked, and he was off to India.

When Kent returned, he gave a report of his trip to the houses during their weekly chapter meetings. In the midst of their usual cussing, drinking, and dirty-joke-telling, Kent shared story after story of young Indian students whose lives were transformed by Jesus Christ. The responses to his presentations were so positive that he was able to recruit and lead a weekly evangelistic Bible study in each of the three houses and saw a number of men come to Christ. It turned out that Kent was really the only light in their darkness; if he had never taken the time (or shown the boldness) to ask these fraternities for support, that mini-revival may have never taken place.

He could have taken the holier-than-thou approach, turned up his nose, and spouted, "I shall not soil my hands with the filthy lucre of these infidels!" Billy Sunday, the crusade evangelist from the 1920s, felt differently. He said, "I'll take the devil's money and I'll wash it in the blood, and then spend it on the Kingdom!" *Interesting*

If you won't ask for or receive gifts from non-Christians, then I have a question for you: How do *you know* who is and isn't a Christian? Personally, I refuse to play Holy Spirit and be the decider as to who is or isn't saved. I encourage Christian workers to ask *every* person they *Interesting* know to join their team. Who knows, some of those appointments might transition into a Gospel presentation!

Once again let's review how Nehemiah and Jesus dealt with this controversial concept of asking for and/or receiving support from supposed "non-believers."

1. NEHEMIAH

At the time, King Artaxerxes was the most powerful man on the planet, but most scholars would say he was not a believer. Nevertheless, Nehemiah prayed and risked his life by asking the King to support his physical and spiritual rebuilding project back in Jerusalem (Nehemiah 2:1-9). Nehemiah must have found favor with the King as a result of his life and service. Consequently, Artaxerxes gave him everything he asked for — and more.

2. JESUS

According to Luke 8:1-3, God in the flesh was supporting Himself and His ministry through ongoing support from individuals. Whether or not He *asked* for the support, the text doesn't say. It *does* list some supporters: "Mary (called Magdalene)…; Joanna the wife of Chuza, the manager of Herod's household; Susanna; and many others." Most focus on Mary's questionable past and *how* she may have acquired her money (possibly in her B.C. prostitute days?). Instead, ask yourself where Joanna got the funds to give to Jesus? Probably from her husband's salary, which was paid by Herod! Was Jesus actually receiving support that came from this ungodly dictator whom He knew would have a hand in killing Him? Apparently so!

NOTE: *Just to comfort your mind, I probably would not ask someone for support if I knew they had acquired their assets illegally or immorally.*

thank goodness!

27

UNDERFUNDED STAFF

What to do now?

I had to turn away from the horrific, gruesome, agonizingly drawn out execution scene of the ancient Scottish hero William Wallace in the movie *Braveheart*. Yes, I wanted my teenage sons to see this man's courage and perseverance, but did Mel Gibson have to show five full minutes of indescribable anguish and torment?

It may sound overdramatic, but I have seen numerous Christian workers over the years experience this kind of slow, torturous death — not physically, but financially and emotionally. Their support team may have been strong and vigorous at one time, but for whatever reason, it began a long, painful descent into "support-raising hell."

Or just as common is the worker who never makes it to 100 percent of his budget and then silently endures the accompanying embarrassment and pressures. Life, marriage, and ministry remain under constant stress because of financial shortfalls. Then questions begin to flood in like: "Is God *really* calling us to continue with this ministry that requires us to raise our support?" Exiting staff always give "reasons" for leaving, but more times than not, an unspoken but core rationale is under-funding.

What should you do if you are under-funded and below budget? You might have someone you are reporting to who has fallen into the "denial ditch" and acts as if all their staff members are doing just fine. Some macho executive types choose the other extreme by coldly administering the "all or nothing" ultimatum to their under-funded staff — who typically are drowning in hopelessness and bitterness. Instead of just twisting in the wind, here are three proactive steps you can take:

1. GET THE RIGHT TRAINING

Some organizations try to "subsidize" under-funded staff in the short term, but this is like putting a band-aid on cancer. Instead of getting a hand out of a fish each day just to survive, why not learn how to fish? Make sure you get the best support-raising training available. That's foundational.

2. FIND THE RIGHT COACH

If you are struggling in support raising, find a mature, fully-funded co-worker who can encourage and troubleshoot, but also has enough backbone to ask tough personal questions. The coach needs to go with you on some support appointments, as well as have specific weekly accountability with you.

3. ESTABLISH THE RIGHT FINISH LINE

You are going to have to ask your supervisor for adequate time off to pack out your weeks with face-to-face appointments. You need to firmly focus your goals and efforts on a challenging, but realistic, finish line. You, your coach, even prospective donors all need to urgently work and pray toward getting to 100 percent by that deadline.

If these steps have been taken and you're still not fully funded, then and only then, would I encourage you and your supervisor to set aside some time to do a complete evaluation of your support-raising efforts and results and try to prayerfully determine whether this really is God's best place of service for you. As hard as it is to cut someone loose, most of us would prefer a quick and painless death to a slow torturous one.

NOTE: *Exiting staffers always remember how you tried to help them as well as how you transitioned them out. Kindness, compassion, and empathy go a long way.*

28

SUBSIDIZING STAFF SALARIES

Does it help or hurt?

The leaders of a particular Christian organization were so anxious to get their new staff to their ministry assignments that they held an emergency meeting on how they could bypass the sometimes long and laborious support-raising process. The president (who was on salary) proposed the re-routing of a $150,000 gift to subsidize new staff salaries. The HR director (also on salary) quickly calculated the percentages and yelled excitedly, "We can cover 60 percent of their first year salary, 30 percent of the second, and by the third they should all be at full support!" A regional director (who'd never gotten to 75 percent in her own support efforts) chimed in, "This should be no problem. Along with their 'on campus' ministry we can give each staffer up to 10 hours a week to work on support. Two or three years of that will be plenty of time to wean them off subsidies and have their *own* team."

I've seen this scenario unfold with many organizations—usually followed a few years later by regret. I once fell into this same trap because we so desperately wanted to expand our ministry and searched for shortcuts to quick "success." What we later realized was that shortcuts only short-*circuit* and that we all — regardless of how well-intentioned — reap what we sow.

Because I've almost never seen a subsidized person get to 100 percent of his own support, below are three reasons why, as we say in the South, "this dog won't hunt."

1. IT BUILDS AN UNHEALTHY DEPENDENCE

Our motive may be to help, but a subtle, even deadly side effect to subsidizing staff can be a debilitating reliance upon the organization and its ever-decreasing "general fund." Maybe we ought to develop our staff like we do our children: Don't do *anything* for them they can do for themselves.

2. IT ATTRACTS AND DEVELOPS THE WRONG KIND OF STAFF

Instead of raising solid, independent, world-changers who yearned to pioneer and establish ministries in the face of opposition and struggle, we were attracting and raising weaker staff who were hoping for a handout and making excuses why they weren't seeing significant ministry results. And what a coincidence that many subsidized personnel felt "led" to leave staff once the subsidies disappeared!

3. IT LIMITS (NOT EXPANDS) THE SIZE OF YOUR STAFF

It boils down to whether you have a centralized or decentralized philosophy of staff funding. Does one ministry executive constantly go back to the same major donors attempting to keep the "supply train" pumped up, or do you spread the task around, helping each staffer feel the *full* weight of raising support? The ministries that are exploding right now are the ones that truly understand "franchising" and give their regional and local staff *maximum* ownership and responsibility — including fundraising.

For us, it wasn't until a gutsy businessman stood up at a board meeting one day and proclaimed, "If new staff can't go out and, from scratch, raise their entire support, how in the world can we expect them to launch and develop a successful campus ministry? Raising their support is not only essential to their preparation, I believe it ought to be a pre-requisite for even coming on our staff!" Wow. That was the last day we ever paid any subsidies.

NOTE: *There may be certain scenarios where you truly believe subsidizing a staff person for a short (or even long) period of time is the wisest way to go. Just pray, get counsel, and proceed cautiously. But, take the long look and understand you may very well be setting a precedent that might have long-term implications.*

Section V

Six Relationships to Nurture

29

SUPPORT-RAISING RELATIONSHIPS

The ones that matter most

1. GOD

Jesus said in John 15:5, *"Apart from me you can do nothing."* We come to Him to find our calling, motivation, and vision. Ask the Lord to fill you with His Spirit, courage, and words. Ask Him to go before you to soften the hearts of your hearers. We cannot do what *only* God can do, but He will not do what He has asked *us* to do. So petition and believe God for big things. Remember, you can honor Him by the magnitude of your requests.

2. PARENTS

Do you remember how your parents responded when you told them you were going into ministry and were required to raise your entire support from scratch? As children, we are required to *obey* our parents, but as adults we are to *honor* them for a lifetime. If we humbly approach our parents and listen to their questions, counsel, and concerns, we will likely receive their blessing and encouragement.

3. SPOUSE

Both husband and wife should be in agreement when deciding to go into ministry and raising support. Praying together, getting counsel, and proceeding as a team is critical for harmony and successful support raising and ministry. You might be satisfied at living at 80 percent of your budget, but it might breed discontentment or resentment in the heart of your spouse toward you, the ministry, or even God. Getting to and staying at 100 percent support can take some stress out of a marriage and is a great way to say, "I love you."

4. CHILDREN

When I speak at Christian colleges full of missionary kids, their attitudes toward support raising are usually either incredibly positive or largely negative. Don't underestimate how your words, actions, and attitudes toward money, support raising, and ministry directly affect your children over the course of their lives. Here is the litmus test:

- Do you view living on support as a blessing or a necessary evil?
- Are you thankful to God and your supporters or are you a complainer?
- Have you raised enough to *really* take care of your family?

If you have a healthy perspective, your children probably will too.

5. PASTOR

Get counsel from your pastor as you consider full-time ministry and support raising. He's probably never been asked to join someone's personal monthly support team. You be the first. See if he will guide you as to who to approach in the church. Ask him to be an advocate for you to the congregation and missions committee. Keep him regularly informed of your personal and ministry progress and needs. Build a track record of credibility and faithfulness with your pastor.

6. FRIENDS

Don't try to do it all yourself. This is "friendraising," not just fundraising. By asking your friends to pray, invest, and build your network, you'll develop in them a long-term loyalty and ownership in you and your ministry. You're not just looking for supporters, but teammates. If, over the course of your life and ministry, you stick with them, most all of them will stick with you.

By the way, why were we put on this earth? For relationships. Let's glorify God by fulfilling the purpose for which we were created. Support raising affords us many, many opportunities to do so.

NOTE: *The following chapters expand on each of these vital relationships you need to maintain and cultivate. The one I do not address is the one with your children. Just please know your spirit and attitude about support raising will forever impact the way your kids will view support raising — and ministry.*

30

GOD

Your motivation in all things

E arly in my Christian life I wanted to be A-plus in *every* area of my
life. An A-plus husband and father, A-plus disciple, A-plus prayer
warrior, A-plus Bible scholar, A-plus evangelist and disciple-maker,
and the list went on. I set very specific and challenging daily goals in
each area to make sure I was on track and recording my impressive
achievements. I don't know whether I've just mellowed out, or if my
definition of "success" has changed, but I've gradually shifted from
striving for an A-plus in every category to simply pass-fail!

Lest you think I'm the only one who has backslidden into mediocrity
and compromise, let me tell you about a friend of mine who is a prominent
speaker and author. He too used to go into overkill each time he plotted
his annual goals. But now, in his latter years, he allots only two seconds
to write his objectives for the next 12 months. Each year it consists of
the same three words: DON'T SCREW UP! I'm pretty confident the
Lord would want you and I to aspire to greater things than that, but I
will say that how a person *finishes* their life says so much more about
them than how they *began* it. And you don't have to get too far down
the road to realize our earthly journey is more like a marathon than a
100-yard dash.

At the core, though, to *every* single area of my life is my relationship
with God. And the *only* place I find any sustaining purpose, zeal, or
motivation to accomplish *anything* is from Him. In John 15, Jesus said
it plainly, "Apart from Me, you can do nothing." Zippo. Zero. The big
goose egg! I'm a fool for even entertaining the thought of relying on
my own *supposed* intelligence, gifts, or skills. My nose is flat because
every time I've chosen self-reliance over abiding in Christ, I fall right
on my face!

What does this abbreviated diary of mid-life confessions have to do with personal support raising? Consider this progression of thought:

1. SUPPORT RAISING IS SPIRITUAL

It's not about technique, personality, or even experience. God is the only one who can turn a heart and cause it to want to give. Yes, God does it — but He chooses to work through us to accomplish this. If I'm not following the Lord and filled with His Spirit, the very *last* thing I can do (or will do!) is pick up the phone to make an appointment. And if I'm spiritually empty, there's no way I can sit across from someone and pretend I am an ambassador of Jesus Christ.

2. SUPPORT RAISING IS SPIRITUAL WARFARE

Why has God designed it such that we should raise support to do the ministry? It's one of the greatest challenges of my life and sometimes feels like a daily — even hourly — battle. And if I've had a long day of support appointments, I don't reward myself with chocolate cake and some late-night television with "questionable" content. Proverbs 4:23 commands us to "watch over our heart with all diligence, for from it flow the springs of life." Support raising *is a battle, and* unless I keep my mind and heart fixed on the love and power of Christ, I will be a victim rather than victor.

3. SUPPORT RAISING IS SPIRITUAL WARFARE WITH SATAN

I believe Satan intensifies his attacks during this critical and vulnerable period of our life. 1 Peter 5:8 warns us, "Watch out for your great enemy, the devil. He prowls around like a roaring lion, looking for someone to devour." Understand that now you have moved up to the top of his "most wanted" list, his goal is not just to distract you but to *devour* you! Consider this: What if the devil could get a wedge into your life at this critical juncture and keep you from reaching or maintaining your 100 percent level of support? Think of *all* the lives you would not touch for Christ because the enemy was able to "sideline" you. Bottom line: the strength of my *public* support raising is directly tied to the strength of my *private* relationship with God.

NOTE: *For more on this topic, see Chapter 55.*

31

PARENTS

A source of blessing

I have wanted to write this letter for decades. Why? Because I've seen a multitude of parents over the years misunderstand — and even oppose — their sons or daughters who feel God's calling into ministry and support raising. Ironically, I've heard more than one mission conference speaker claim the greatest obstacle to completing world evangelization is Christian parents! They certainly want their children to go to church, obey the law, and abstain from smoking and drinking, but some will beg, borrow, or steal to keep their son or daughter from doing something *truly* foolish with their life — like go overseas as a missionary!

Deep down, all of us want (and need!) our parents' blessing in this life. Some wise parents give it willingly, some begrudgingly, and some never offer it at all. If I could pass a note to the parents of every Christian worker who raises support, here is what I would include:

Dear Parents of Support Raisers,

My wife and I are now the parents of young adults, and we're working hard to help them become self-sufficient. As you may know, transitioning them *out* of the nest and into good jobs with incomes to cover ALL of their expenses can sometimes be a frustrating, drawn-out, experience. That's one of the main reasons we send them to (and pay for) college — so they can have a good foundation from which to support themselves for the rest of their lives.

When your sons or daughters came home and informed you they were headed into full-time ministry, it may have been a surprise. But, when they mentioned they would be required to raise their *own* salary, you may have gone into shock! Did you think, "Who are these people that take advantage of naïve Christians by bringing them into their organizations, working them to death, and expecting them to pay their bills by begging from others?" I know. My businessman dad felt the same way and was initially embarrassed by me, his fanatical son, who (he hoped) would someday grow out of this monastic phase.

These thoughts might help you understand why the organization asks your sons or daughters to raise support, and why they agreed to do it:

1. SUPPORT RAISING IS BIBLICAL

The Levites in the Old Testament, the Apostle Paul, even Jesus (Luke 8:1-3) lived off the support of others. If the Son of God was willing to humble himself by being financially dependent upon God and others, shouldn't we be too?

2. SUPPORT RAISING IS THE GREATEST PREPARATION FOR MINISTRY

It requires faith, hard work, and perseverance to be successful in ministry. Those qualities, and more, are developed and refined during the support-raising time. You will definitely see a deepening of their character through this process.

3. SUPPORT RAISING IS NOT BEGGING

Actually, we're inviting others to be ministry partners with us. In the course of them investing, through us, in the Great Commission, we also build lifelong friendships with them. I secretly feel sorry for those Christian workers who do not have a team of 40-60 couples and churches regularly praying for and supporting them. For me and my family, we wouldn't want to live any other way.

4. SUPPORT RAISING IS FOR BRAVE AND BOLD VISIONARIES

About 70 percent of the world's full-time Christian workers are "faith missionaries" who raise their own support. Christian workers drawing a guaranteed monthly salary check is primarily a western, denominational idea developed over the last 100 years. You ought to be extremely proud of your son or daughter for taking on a challenge that few are willing or able to take on. Our world has desperate needs and it is *your* offspring who is determined to be part of the solution rather than the problem.

My dad is now one of our most enthusiastic and proudest supporters, and it will mean the world to your sons or daughters for you to get behind them with *all* your heart. They may or may not be in full-time ministry forever, but they will never forget you cheering them on during one of the greatest challenges of their lives.

NOTE: *For more on this topic, see Chapter 57.*

32

SPOUSES

Teammates for life

S cenario 1: A man with a stable, high-paying position has a spiritual renewal in his life and feels called to a full-time ministry that will mean leaving his job and raising support. As he excitedly shares the news with his wife, she sits and stews in stony silence before blurting out, "When I married you, this wasn't part of the deal!"

Scenario 2: A couple has been accepted by a mission agency, gone through the support training, and begun appointments with potential donors. After several frustrating rejections, the husband turns to his wife and says, "You're better at this than me. Why don't *you* just raise the support we need?"

Scenario 3: A dynamic youth worker marries a businessman from her church. As she goes out to build a support team, people raise their eyebrows and say, "Why are *you* raising support? Your husband has a good salary," thus making her feel like she and her ministry aren't legitimate.

These are just three samplings from the myriad of obstacles couples can face as they engage in the challenging task of support raising. If you are the husband or the wife of the primary support raiser in your family, then this letter is for you:

> Dear Spouse of a Support Raiser,
>
> You may be thrilled that your spouse has chosen to go into ministry and raise support — or you may not be! Don't feel alone if you have questions, struggles, or fears about raising and living on support. We all do. If any family or friends look down on you or your spouse for the ministry path you've taken, don't let them discourage you. In spite of how our culture pressures us to conform, you are — by

living on support — being obedient to God: *"The Lord has commanded that those who preach the Gospel should receive their living from the Gospel."* (1 Corinthians 9:14, NIV)

My hope, though, is that you will not view yourself as simply the *spouse* of a support raiser, but rather a *co*-support raiser working as a teammate, standing shoulder to shoulder.

So, whether or not you are officially involved in the same ministry as your support-raising spouse, here are some ideas on how you can help:

- Set up appointments
- Go on appointments
- Keep all the support-raising information and records organized
- Pray for/with your spouse
- Pray for your supporters
- Put together newsletters
- Make/send gifts to supporters
- Periodically call supporters *and* their spouses
- Host supporters in your home
- Create and maintain a website or blog about your ministry/family
- Remember birthdays and anniversaries of supporters and their children
- Encourage and reward your spouse's hard work
- Take on some of your spouse's chores
- Help stay on budget

Bottom Line: Attitude is everything!

Maintain faith and hope during the tough times. Ask God to give you a heart full of desire, not just duty. Your spouse will be overjoyed by seeing that you've moved from the "ought to" to the "want to" in the support-raising activities. Ecclesiastes 4:9 is so true: "Two are better than one, because they have a good return for their labor." That's true for marriage, ministry, and raising support. There will be tough times during the support raising, but focus on maintaining faith and hope in God — and your spouse!

NOTE: *For more on this topic, see Chapter 54.*

33

PASTORS

Giving endorsement

As a former pastor, I still remember all the various demands and pressures put on me by so many. Over the years, I've had the privilege of interacting with thousands of different pastors from almost every denominational and non-denominational stripe. My respect for the shepherds of local churches is off the charts. But as it relates to the topic of support raising, I have noticed some who fit into these "less than encouraging" categories:

1. THE "HIGH CONTROL" PASTORS

They create strict rules that prevent anyone from approaching *their* members for financial support. Or they make a support raiser choose either to ask the missions committee for support *or* approach members, but not both. Or if members do give to the support raiser, they must do it *through* the church.

2. THE "DENOMINATION ONLY" PASTORS

Only those who are going into full-time ministry with *their* denomination get help from the church. It's not quite as bad as leprosy, but a person can feel pushed out and ostracized from his own local body just because God has called him to work with a different group. That hurts.

3. THE "NO PARA-CHURCH" PASTORS

The support raiser's ministry is not legitimate if it's not through (and under the authority of) a local church. These pastors only see the little "c" (local church), not the big "C" (whole Body of Christ), and they believe *all* giving must be *only* to the local church. Consequently, they make Christian workers feel like they're outside of God's will.

4. THE "FIT MY CATEGORIES" PASTORS

It's fantastic that churches are specifically thinking through *how* they want to disperse their giving, but sometimes God does not fit into those tidy little categories and percentages. Priority must be given to a person who is raised up from that church — almost regardless of what ministry they've chosen. I concur with the well-known statement: The measure of a church is not its seating capacity, but its sending capacity.

> Dear Pastor of a Support Raiser,
>
> You have a thousand things swirling around you and don't have time for some armchair critic like me pestering you, but I am curious. What if, after being unanimously affirmed to be the pastor of your church, the head of the personnel committee turned to you and said, "Great! Now, as soon as you go out and raise your support, you can begin your ministry here?" How would you have responded? That's the exact circumstance faced by myriads of Christian workers. They can't start their ministry until they go out, from scratch, and raise their *entire* monthly budget (usually including all taxes, insurances, and even a hefty administration fee).
>
> I wish you could hear the numerous tearful, heart-wrenching stories of dedicated believers who have told me how they felt called into ministry and, after excitedly going to their pastor or missions committee for a blessing and support, walked away instead feeling betrayed and abandoned. As a result, many never made it into ministry, but almost all struggle with lifelong resentment toward their church and/ or pastor.
>
> I appeal to you today to be different. I know church finances can be tight, but why not adopt an "open hand" policy toward God, toward your members, and toward those who feel called to full-time ministry in your congregation?

I call the latter type:

THE "WIDER VIEW" PASTORS

They understand we have a big God who is using all kinds of people though all kinds of groups doing all kinds of great works all over the world. They purposely and actively search throughout their congregation to recruit, raise, and send out workers they can person ally and corporately support, pray over, and encourage. They prove their endorsement of this worker by lending their credibility and contacts to help them be successful. These pastors believe God's heavenly bank (described in Philippians 4:19) is nice and full and *never* in need of bailouts or stimulus packages! Lastly, they do not subscribe to the "diminishing pie" theory whereby God has limited resources and doesn't have enough to fully fund the needs of the local church along with the thousands of para-church ministries and agencies around the planet.

34

FRIENDS

Providing partnership

Most people in ministry who raise their own support view others as either givers or prayers. Why not take a minute and look at your contact list and think through three or four individuals who might want to do more? I'm sure there a few who, deep down, would love to be a full-fledged partner with you as you begin this exciting journey of getting to full support.

Question: Why are there so few laypeople filling this kind of critical role?

Answer: Because we have never asked them!

King Solomon understood the power of two, and even better, the power of three: *"Two are better than one because they have a good return for their labor. ... A cord of three strands is not quickly torn apart."* (Ecclesiastes 4:9, 12b)

One definition of a good manager is someone who knows how to get things done *through* others. So why just add when you can multiply? Pray and ask one, two, three (or more) people to team up with you to take on and conquer this challenge. But *you* must give them a vision for it — along with a job description.

> Dear Friend of a Support Raiser,
>
> I know you want to give to your friend who is raising support for their ministry. I know you want to pray, too. Secretly, you may even want to be out there in full-time ministry actually *doing* what your friend is doing! But there is another way you can truly partner with him and play an essential and strategic role. You can be a key man (or woman), helping him more quickly get to full support.

Here are some practical suggestions:

1. BECOME THEIR SUPPORT-RAISING PARTNER

You can do this by coming onto his monthly support team, setting up support appointments for him, going on those appointments, and verbally sharing *why* you are giving, setting up small group meetings, and, of course, praying for and with him.

2. CREATE A "STEERING COMMITTEE"

This is a carefully selected, short-term group that knows the Christian worker and that's committed to meeting *each* month until the worker is at *full* support. They give, network and share contacts, set up meetings, brainstorm ideas, pray, and help hold the worker accountable for his support-raising efforts. (See the next chapter for more help on this.)

3. USE YOUR "TRIANGLES OF TRUST"

I believe there are several people in your life who love and trust you enough that they would *personally* meet with your support-raising friend to listen to his ministry vision and financial goals — if you would ask. Why would they meet with someone they don't even know? Just because *you* asked them.

Thanks for your willingness to join your friend and carry some of the load on this walk up a tough mountain. When the two of you finally get to the top, I know it will be a grand celebration to see that Christian worker report to his ministry assignment fully funded. I promise, your friend will never ever forget the kindness and partnership you extended during the first (and toughest) part of the journey.

Section VI

Five Strategies to Follow

35

RECRUIT TEAMMATES

The power of building a steering committee

J osh and Katie felt lonely and isolated. They had applied and been accepted to a well-known youth ministry, which then gave them a book to read about support raising and told them to report to their assignment when they raised their full budget. Six months later and stuck at 18 percent, they sat in a room and silently stared at each other.

"Why are we trying to do this all by ourselves?" Katie finally said. "Why don't we get some of our friends involved? I bet a number of them would want to do more than just give."

Immediately they started brainstorming such things as who they would invite to be part of a steering committee, what their roles would be, and how often they should meet. Discouragement gave way to hope as they started calling and inviting various friends to attend the first monthly meeting of what they called their "Go Team."

At their first meeting, Katie shared two key verses that provided the rationale for starting the group:

ECCLESIASTES 4:9-10

"Two are better than one, for they have a good return for their labor. If either of them falls, the other will lift him up. But woe to the one who falls when there is not another to lift him up."

HEBREWS 10:24-25

"And let us consider how to stimulate one another to love and good deeds, not forsaking our own assembling together, as is the habit of some, but encouraging one another, and all the more, as you see the day drawing near."

After thanking everyone for coming, Josh went over the job descriptions for the five couples and three singles who had driven in from around the greater Philadelphia area. He framed it as "Four Ways

You Can Help Us Get to 100 Percent Support." These 13 willing and able friends already were on their monthly support team, but there were a few *other* strategic ways they could help get this couple to their inner-city ministry quickly — and fully funded:

1. COMMIT TO PRAY REGULARLY

Josh and Katie promised to send out a weekly email to the Go Team that included prayer requests, along with the names of people they were approaching. The team was to pray for boldness and sensitivity for them, but also openness and generosity on the part of the potential supporters.

2. BRAINSTORM FOR NEW CONTACTS

Every member was supposed to bring to each meeting at least five new names (and contact info) for Josh and Katie to follow up on. As a group they would share those names, talk about the best way to approach them, and pray by name over the new list.

3. SET UP SUPPORT APPOINTMENTS *FOR* THEM

In addition to just thinking of new names, each Go Team member was to try to actually set up at least one appointment every other week for Josh and Katie. The members were trying to create a "Triangle of Trust" whereby they would ask friends and associates to meet with the ministry couple. Why? Just because they asked!

4. ENCOURAGE AND HOLD THEM ACCOUNTABLE

The team helped Josh and Katie set up monthly, weekly, and daily goals on how many calls and appointments they were to make. The couple reported back each month on how they did on their goals and on the results. They also shared their personal struggles. Each month, the meeting ended with everyone praying over Josh and Katie and for their efforts the next 30 days.

And how long did their Go Team meet? Until they got to 100 percent support, which was about four months after they started it!

36

UTILIZE TECHNOLOGY

Facebook: A support raiser's new best friend

W e ask participants in our SRS Bootcamps to bring the names and contact information of 200-600 friends or acquaintances they've made during their lifetime. Without exception, there are a few trainees who can't seem to come up with more than 80 or so names. If I were just a tad meaner I would mock them, saying, "You're 40 years old and want to go into full-time Christian work? So, you love the ministry. It's just people that you hate!"

I'd never say that, of course, but there's a sad bit of truth in my sarcasm. Ministry is the people business. If we haven't spent time reaching out to others in our B.F.M. (Before Full-Time Ministry) days, what makes us think we'll flip some magical switch inside our brains that instantly transforms us into servers who love the multitudes, giving our lives away in nurturing relationships? As we say in Arkansas, "Ain't gonna happen!"

But I don't want to come down too hard on the "Mr. Bootcamper with only 80 names guy" because he's just doing what almost every support raiser does starting out. It's not that they hate anyone; the problem is they summarily cross off their prospect list the names of hundreds of folks they haven't seen in years. You see, of the approximately one thousand people you've met or known in some measure during your short stay on this planet, you've probably stayed in touch with only about 60 of them. And the only people with the guts (or penchant for rejection) to actually call any of the "neglected" 940 are Amway or insurance salesmen!

Well, a 20-something Harvard dropout named Mark Zuckerberg has changed all of that. Instead of it being weird or awkward to reconnect with your fifth grade Girl Scout friend or your ninth grade lab partner, it's OK — even cool — to do so. How did Zuckerberg pull it off? In 2004 he created a simple computer program to communicate with some of his college buddies. When it caught on at other campuses, he opened it up to all colleges, then all high schoolers, and finally the whole world!

Someone recently told me Facebook was the third-largest country in the world! My research confirmed that Facebook is now the largest and fastest growing social network anywhere, with hundreds of millions of active users who spend billions of minutes a day cruising the site for more friends. Here are four quick ways Facebook can become a support raiser's new best friend:

1. RESURRECT YOUR "NAMESTORM LIST"

Rethink all the hundreds of names you conveniently "forgot" about from your past lives and go back and write each one down. Don't leave anyone off!

2. BEFRIEND THEM ON FACEBOOK

Search for and ask each to be your friend. Virtually everyone says yes because the measure of popularity on Facebook is *how many* friends you accumulate. Enjoy reconnecting, sharing memories, and old pictures. I have my 14-year-old daughter right now going through every one of my friends and recording their name and email address (and other pertinent info) and will be adding them to my email newsletter list.

3. JOIN OR START AFFINITY GROUPS AND INVITE OLD FRIENDS

Your friends have joined a number of the thousands of Facebook clubs/groups with interests ranging from sports teams to school classes to hobbies. Jump in and have some fun.

4. BUILD RAPPORT AND PREPARE TO ASK

Pick and choose friends you want to go deeper with. As you share your life and ministry, it opens up spiritual discussions and opportunities. Then when you set up your next round of support-raising trips, these "old-new" friends will be primed to see you and will listen closely to the voice and heart they remembered from many moons ago.

NOTE: *MySpace.com, Classmates.com, Plaxo.com, and LinkedIn.com are other examples of social and professional networks to help reconnect you to your old friends.*

37

MULTIPLY CONTACTS

Asking for referrals is key to expanding your list

Olga was a 24-year-old campus staff worker we met during the year our family spent reaching out to college students in Ukraine. She was later assigned to come to America and raise $2,700 in new monthly support that would cover her budget and that of two other national staff. She knew no one here and had only a 21-day visa. So a fellow staff person here made a deal with Olga. He would give her 40 "referrals" to start her support-raising activities if she would give him 40 new ones on her way out of the country.

And that's exactly what happened. Olga was so motivated that she raised the entire $2,700 in new monthly support using *only* referrals (and referrals of referrals) and gave that staff guy 40 new ones before her trip home. She was a woman on a mission from God!

For some people, asking for referrals is unnecessary because they have hundreds of people from different stages of life who they can go back to and invite onto their team. But some will *have* to pursue a strategy of asking for referrals to get to 100 percent support. If so, here are some thoughts:

1. FIRST, EXPAND YOUR THINKING

Come on now. Have you *really* worked hard at namestorming every person you've ever known (or even met) and put them down on your list? Again, go back and scour all your school annuals, church directories, hometown phonebooks, etc.

2. HAVE A SENSE OF URGENCY

Like Olga, are you willing to go *anywhere* and talk to *anyone* about your ministry and coming on your support team? Some are too proud — or too lazy — to do *whatever* it takes to get to their ministry assignment quickly and fully funded.

3. PREPARE AND PRACTICE

Don't shoot from the hip when asking for referrals. Craft a script and role play it with friends. Get feedback and practice again. Make the first 10 appointments with people who will be favorable toward your request for referrals.

4. ASK EVERY PERSON FOR REFERRALS

Invite *every person you meet with* to join your regular support team. And *after* they have made a decision (yes or no), tell them there's one more way they can help — by suggesting friends of theirs you might meet with who also care about reaching out for Christ. If they resist, then back away and don't press it.

5. HELP THEM THINK OF NAMES

It may be they're not resisting, they just need their memory jogged a bit. If possible, do a little advance homework. If they are part of a church, small group, or club, you might mention these one at a time to see if names come to their mind. If they give you names, ask if they have phone numbers and addresses handy.

6. BE POSITIVE AND THANKFUL

Expect to get a good response. Believe in God and that you and your ministry are worth a significant investment. Be thankful to the Lord and to each person who trusts you enough to give referrals to you. Treat each one with great care.

NOTE: *You can make some big mistakes if you don't prepare and approach people properly. Before you ask anyone for a referral, please carefully read this detailed five-page article online:*

supportraisingsolutions.org/wp-content/uploads/2013/05/referrals.pdf

38

COMMUNICATE WITH EXCELLENCE

Newsletters can make you — or break you!

I get numerous ministry newsletters each week from various Christian workers around the world. A few are good, more are bad, and some — real ugly! Let's look at them in reverse order:

THE UGLY

1. DISTRESS SIGNAL

"We're going under unless *you* give!" may work once, but doing it again raises huge questions about our ability to raise and manage funds.

2. SUBTLE ASK

Instead of asking folks face to face to join our team, we slip in hints in the prayer requests, or even worse, we include envelopes to do "the ask" for us. And the ultimate manipulation? Putting a stamp on it to "guilt us" into giving.

3. ALL FAMILY NEWS

As excited as we are about Tommy's baseball or Katie's soccer, our supporters are not investing in us to find out sports scores. Have a small family section, but focus on the ministry's progress and changed lives.

4. NO NEWS IS BAD NEWS

A ministry update *just* once or twice a year communicates that we really don't care about our supporters or their investment. A few years of that and we can say "aloha" to our support team.

These ugly ones normally go straight to the shredder.

THE BAD

1. SEA OF WORDS

A newsletter that's all text quickly overwhelms the reader. If it has no pictures and very little white space, it won't have many readers, either. Give your newsletter more of a *USA Today* feel rather than the 10,000-word front page of the *New York Times* feel.

2. TOO MUCH DETAIL

Research tells us our readers will give us 11 seconds. They look at pictures, captions, bullet points, and the postscript. To draw them into the text itself, it better be short — and powerful.

3. INSIDER SPEAK

Don't use religious jargon or acronyms; instead, spell everything out in simple language.

4. POOR TALK

Sharing pictures of the old van with 200,000 miles on it, sharing about how neighbors gave clothes to our kids, or explaining that health insurance has gone up makes us look like beggars and robs us of the honor and calling of our ministry role.

These bad ones normally go straight to my file folder on how *not* to do newsletters.

THE GOOD

1. GET PERMISSION

If you've *asked* if they would like to receive a newsletter, then they won't view it as junk mail. And if they aren't supporters yet, this can open the door for a future appointment.

2. STANDARD OF EXCELLENCE

A well-written, well-designed newsletter (color increases readership 60 percent) says everything about us — and our ministry.

3. ALL ABOUT VISION

Make sure the headlines, pictures, stories, and prayer requests stay *focused* on the vision of the ministry.

4. CHANGED LIVES

Each newsletter should include a picture and a story of a transformed life. It doesn't always have to be someone *we* led to Christ, but a person impacted by our ministry. Our supporters are making spiritual investments, and they *want* to see the dividends.

These good ones normally go straight to our family devotional time the next morning to help build vision and passion in our children's hearts.

Bottom line: The purpose of newsletters is to share *vision* and *changed lives.*

39

THINK LONG TERM

How to recession-proof your finances

W ell, the title is a misnomer. We never totally "recession-proof" anything. I'm sure Job felt very safe and secure until disaster wiped him out. In fact, if I get arrogant about how "recession-proof" my finances are I might find the God I'm supposedly serving actually *opposing* me! 1 Peter 5:5b: "God is opposed to the proud, but gives grace to the humble." Hmmm ... God vs. my so-called financial "security"? God wins every time!

If one ditch is pride, the other one is denial. Some Christian workers don't attempt to understand or track with the national economy, financial trends, or even personal money management. Is it a waste of time or unspiritual to do so? Yes, we can turn our backs on the world of finance and proclaim ourselves "holy ones," choosing not to "soil our hands with filthy lucre." But down the road, we may wish we had paid a tad more attention.

Whether or not these tough economic times have impacted your level of support or financial stability, why not view it as a "wake-up call" from God to build a strong, healthy, long-term support team and financial base? But there are no magic formulas to help you weather the storms of our economy. All I have to offer are the old-fashioned, tried and true basics:

1. LET'S GET BIBLICAL

When my wife and I were in a wreck in Mexico 20 years ago, we incurred seemingly insurmountable medical bills and our finances went into a tailspin. We went back to the Scriptures to see what God taught about the absolute necessity of us giving sacrificially, destroying debt, saving and investing regularly. We chose to obey and make radical changes in our thinking and finances. The Lord honored it and rescued us. As a result, God led us to adopt the pattern of Joseph, who stored up for seven years to prepare for future years of drought. We copied the ant in Proverbs who worked hard when he had the chance in order to have provisions in season and out. The Bible is amazingly practical about many things — including money!

2. LET'S GET PERSONAL

If you haven't already, go back to EVERY single person who *yes!* supports you and meet with them *face to face*. Heart to heart, review with them the vision God has given you and thank them so much for being willing to invest some of their strategic giving dollars in you and your ministry. Let them know how critical they are as ministry partners and how you're going to do a better job of communicating with them. Right then and there, pray for them, their family, and any other concerns they have. This face-to-face approach creates an "expectations exchange" they will never forget whereby they committed to you and you committed to them. You'll probably be the last place they reduce their giving when the economy tanks again and cutbacks are required.

3. LET'S GET MISSIONAL

If supporters sense that being fully funded is more important to you than fulfilling the Great Commission, they won't stay on your team very long. They want to know your heart and eyes are fixed on the person and purposes of Jesus Christ and that you are working just as hard as they are (in their secular jobs) to bring about eternal change in the lives of people. Thus, your days (and your newsletters!) need to be chock full of tangible ministry activities — and results — letting your supporters know their giving is making a real difference. These "success" stories will re-energize their commitment.

Section VII

Nine Issues for Leaders to Examine

40

BUILDING MORALE

The value of modeling

The movie *Gladiator* opens with the Roman general Maximus leading his troops into battle against a horde of vicious barbarians. While most generals would simply sit on a distant hill observing the conflict, Maximus leads the charge himself, all the while yelling at the top of his lungs, "Stay with me! Staaaay with meeee!" No wonder he never lost a battle — mainly because his men incorporated the same loyalty and bravery their leader had modeled for years. The reason they respected Maximus so much? He never asked them to do *anything* he wasn't willing to do himself.

I've known a few "field generals" like Maximus in Christian ministries — men and women who get their hands dirty by leading the charge rather than sitting at the back pushing buttons and pulling strings. This stark contrast in leadership philosophies plays itself out in support raising, also. Let me explain.

I've received a myriad of phone calls over the years from leaders of Christian ministries whose staff members are struggling with their personal support levels. As I've probed a little deeper, I'll ask that leader if he or she is on personal support. They usually stumble and stutter a bit, saying that it was the board that wanted to pay them a salary or that their schedule is so busy they don't have the time.

At this point I shoot up a quick prayer, take a big gulp, and gently say, "Well, if you want, I can tell you how to turn this whole ship around." I can tell they are all ears at this point. I then proceed to share how they can become a "field general" rather than an "armchair quarterback" by taking the time to raise their entire monthly *personal* support and thus model to their staff members *exactly* what they are asking them to do. After I finish, there's usually a long awkward pause on the line and the conversation winds up pretty quickly and sometimes I don't hear from them again. Not that many CEOs have ever taken me up on that particular suggestion.

You may be in a situation where you raise major dollars and your salary comes from a portion of that total. I understand that arrangement, and it is certainly legitimate. My suggestions below may not apply to all ministry leaders, but I have seen some amazing transformations take place by leaders who have taken this route. I've seen how applying these principles can produce stronger followership, loyalty, and bravery in a staff. Consider these few steps:

1. RAISE YOUR PERSONAL SUPPORT

Understand that just raising organizational money that your salary is taken out of is different than starting from ground zero and putting together a personal, monthly support team. Think about the power of modeling this to your staff by doing what you're asking them to do: Raise 100 percent of their support and stay at 100 percent. That gives you the credibility and moral authority to expect and require your staff to get to and stay at full support.

2. TAKE STAFF OUT ON SUPPORT-RAISING APPOINTMENTS

Don't just tell them, show them how you do it. Can I tell you the main reason people do not come on your staff? It is not because of inferior materials, programs, or personnel. The unspoken reason is almost always because they are afraid (or ignorant of how) to raise support. If you and your staff simply take your recruits on support appointments, it will get them over the hump — big time.

3. NEVER ASK YOUR STAFF TO DO THE "HARD THINGS" THAT YOU'RE NOT WILLING TO DO YOURSELF

I'm sure you've observed Christian workers who are "promoted," moved to headquarters, or get the corner office with the nameplate on the door, and they start to think they're excused from the standards and sacrifices required of the rank-and-file staff members. Even when we assume a place of leadership, we can't give in to the temptation of believing we now deserve special privileges, rights, or perks. It will kill morale and loyalty.

NOTE: *These steps may or may not be possible for you to implement. Pray and evaluate what God would have you do. If the support-raising DNA in your organization is weak, I believe you can "re-create" it by becoming a field general who consistently talks and walks the "Stay with me!" attitude. (More on this in Chapter 49.)*

41

SETTING THE BAR HIGH

For ourselves and others

Why is it taking 12-24 months for many Christian workers to raise their support and get to their assignment? Is it because of poor training, a lack of faith, or a dismal work ethic? Well, maybe. But some of the blame might rest with the person who was staring back at us in the mirror this morning as we brushed our teeth.

Workers come into our organizations full of hope, enthusiasm, and teachableness. If we were to tell them to jump, they'd ask "how high?" on the way up. But instead of inscribing "GO FOR IT!" on the fresh tablet of their heart, we drag them down to the least common denominator by telling them it's fine and normal to raise support in their spare time, to take 24 months, or to just have a few appointments per week.

I once asked a group of seasoned support-raising trainers: "If a new staffer is raising support full-time, what's a reasonable number of appointments we should expect them to have each week?" I was stunned to hear one veteran trainer answer, "I would be happy if they had 6-10 appointments."

I promise I am not trying to shock you or put you in any legalistic shackles, but think with me for a moment. There are six days in a week (take a Sabbath!) with six slots available to schedule appointments: breakfast, mid-morning, lunch, mid-afternoon, dinner, and evening. Be honest with me. If a person works hard on a full-time basis to get to 100 percent budget, how many of those 36 slots each week would be a challenging, but realistic number to fill? I have to believe more than 6-10! I bet the sales people you meet with would not keep their job very long if they only made one or two sales calls a day! Aren't the very people we're approaching for support working 40-, 50-, maybe 60-hour workweeks? I'm not suggesting we become workaholics, but should we not work just as hard at raising our support as the people we're asking to sacrifice for us and our ministry?

Scenario 1: Joe Businessman has dinner with Sam Staffer, who is going to ask him for support. Joe casually inquires, "How many appointments have you had today, Sam?" After a full day, if all Sam can say is, "This is my first," what is Joe going to think?

Scenario 2: Joe Businessman and his wife have Sally Staffer over for dessert one evening to hear about her ministry and financial needs. Curious, Joe again asks, "Sally, it's 8 p.m., and I know you're working on support full-time. Tell me, how many appointments have you had today?" Sally humbly responds, "Well, let's see, my day started early with a 6:30 breakfast, then a 10:30 meeting, an afternoon appointment, and I just finished dinner with an old college friend. I guess that makes you my fifth appointment for today."

You tell me. Which staffer will Joe want to invest in? It's going to be the one who has a sense of urgency, who is on a mission from God, who is working hard morning, noon, and night to get to full support and their Great Commission ministry assignment.

But it's often the organizational leaders, not the new staffers, who lowered the bar to a safe, comfortable "snail-like" pace. I hope you will join me in my frustration and that it would move us to action and change. Let's set the bar high for ourselves and lovingly challenge *and* bring other staff along. If we want them to do hard things, we must set the pace by doing even harder things.

42

FRONT DOOR-BACK DOOR

Why people leave your organization

B radley was nervous when he came into the office, visibly shaken by what he was about to announce to the leadership team. Although he was now a veteran staffer — having served for six years — it had been difficult from day one. He and his family had struggled month after month with their personal support level and his inability to provide for their basic needs. Bradley did not mention any of this, but instead spoke softly of the Lord using certain circumstances, passages, and other's counsel to finally show him God wanted his family to move back to their hometown and for him to join his father's business. He added how much his kids would benefit from such things as being near the grandparents being in a good church youth group.

Scenarios like this play out hundreds of times each month among the nation's ministries that require staff to raise their own funds. And when the departing staff shares that "God is leading them" to another ministry or back into the secular workforce, what are we supposed to say: "No He's not!?"

Many staff members will explain their leaving by listing their frustrations with the organization, leadership, other staff, or their own ministry role. But, as you look deep into their eyes, you might be thinking, "I hear your words, I see your tears. But what is *really* behind all this?" More times than not, we do not feel the freedom to ask that question lest we be accused of judging or badgering them.

The truth is, all of us live in some degree of denial and tend to blame everything and everyone — except ourselves. Professor and author Howard Hendricks believes financial tensions (partly or mainly) cause up to 90 percent of all divorces, and I contend the same is true for most of our departing staff. They may give every reason under the sun why they're moving on, but it usually boils down to support related issues.

Our organization performs "Support-raising Audits" for ministries, anonymously surveying (via a secure Internet site) all their staff members in 12 essential categories and trying to gauge the overall "support raising" health of the ministry. It's designed to shed light on the staff's true feelings and status in this very critical, yet sensitive area. One audit revealed the staff of a particular agency believed 92 percent of their former personnel had left mainly (or partly) due to support-related struggles. Unbelievable! So, as appealing as this ministry's large front door was to attract fresh, excited new staff, the majority of them were destined to head out the back door before long, discouraged or even embittered. Even though our organization provides follow-up consulting to help remedy this situation, a report like this can be sobering for a mission executive to read.

Not all staff or organizations are plagued by this dilemma. But for most, there's an elephant in the living room that no one really wants to admit is there. Let's deal with it and let him out the back door. Then shut it. TIGHT!

43

CROSSING THE RIVER OF DENIAL

Why it's so hard to change ourselves

F lying from London to Nairobi in a 767 is quite an experience. If the expanse of that mammoth plane doesn't take your breath away, peering down on the terrifying terrain will. After gazing at a thousand miles of Sahara Desert, the gigantic and intimidating Nile River suddenly comes into view, cutting a huge swath through the vast African continent. Eyes staring and mind racing, I couldn't imagine someone attempting to cross the Nile, much less the Sahara.

Some call trying to conquer the most fearsome parts of nature "extreme sports." I call it a "death wish!" After failing to jump over a huge canyon on a motorcycle, the daredevil Robbie Knievel explained his actions to a reporter by saying, "Everybody has a calling. This is mine." Yes, everyone has a calling, Robbie, but not everyone is *stupid*!

Standing at the edge of a canyon, a desert, or a gargantuan river like the Nile makes us feel small, inadequate, and overwhelmed. Maybe you've had that exact feeling as you look over the organization you help lead. I know I have. Depression can set in when we get real honest about all the gaps, struggles, dysfunctions, inefficiencies, and lost opportunities we observe. What to do? Where to start? Instead of just sticking our head in the sand or looking for the nearest bridge to jump off, consider these steps:

1. PULL YOUR TEAM TOGETHER

Don't be the Lone Ranger and arrogantly believe your brilliance, personality, and willpower can get you out of the valley and up the mountain. Get your key people away for a day or more, grab a white board, and *really* start with a clean slate. Let them know (maybe for the first time?) that *their* opinions, assessments, and "buy in" are critical to the future success.

2. CONFRONT THE BRUTAL FACTS

This is what Jim Collins (in his book, *Good to Great*) encourages leaders to do *before* they begin to strategize or implement. No need to put on a confident smile and act like you have it all together. Everyone on the team usually knows the truth; they're just waiting for the leader to admit it. So really, truly, listen to them, and try not to let pride and defensiveness get in the way.

3. BRING IN SOME OUTSIDE HELP

We've worked with hundreds of organizations, and we've been able to observe a few things. Most ministries, especially para-church organizations, think they can do everything "in house." Instead of turning to an experienced and objective outsider who can quickly and accurately pinpoint the problems and solutions, they ride their ship right down to its watery grave. Why? Usually to save face or save a buck — or both. Ask God for wisdom to know which things should be handled by your people and which ones should be "farmed out" to specialists.

NOTE: *God can use this unity-building exercise in powerful ways, but our denial will thwart our prospects for healthy change and growth. Go ahead. Cross that river.*

44

PLACING PRIORITY ON TRAINING

It shows you care

B lindsided. That's the only word I can think of to describe my experience. It was supposed to just be a short workshop for the 25 or so staff from the local chapter of an international Christian ministry. But within seconds of my closing prayer, 10-15 crying and emotionally charged young men and women mobbed around me. Their frustrations soon became obvious — stress, feelings of failure, and guilt were not their fault, but were thoughtlessly thrust upon them by their ministry leaders.

For years the directors of this ministry set incredibly high goals for their staff in the areas of trusting God, working hard, and living sacrificially. Normally, these are all excellent values to strive for, but these staff members felt continually pressured to go, go, go and produce results — but without the necessary finances to sustain them. Ongoing unrealistic expectations combined with inadequate funding can gradually rip apart even the sturdiest missionary.

As I questioned these struggling staff members, I discovered the root cause. The leaders of this organization appeared to care more about their outreach programs and numbers of converts than they did the well being and longevity of their team. What was the tragic but true evidence of these mixed up priorities? The staff had received virtually no meaningful training in how to build solid, healthy personal support teams. Their motto of "living by faith" had given way to the tyranny of the urgent as regional and country leaders called for more and more bricks — but with no straw!

Excellent, thorough, and practical support training is essential, but just giving loud *exhortations* without providing detailed *explanations* only produces *frustrations*. Sad to say, here are four pitiful examples of real-life horror stories of over-bearing, but under-nourishing staff leaders and the full extent of their supposed "training" of their staff:

- One ministry just gave each staffer a book to read
- Another just showed them examples of newsletters
- A two-hour orientation was all one group received
- Another gave no training, but cheerfully said, "Give us an update each quarter. We'll pray for you!"

When an organization does not take the time and money to get its staff fully trained in how to put together a stable, long-term support team, it communicates that the leadership really doesn't care about them. Deep down, the directors *know* that lack of funds cause staff to experience personal and marital stress, a questioning of their calling, spiritual disillusionment, and a premature exit from ministry. The ones usually adversely affected the most are the spouses and children who are forced to suffer in silence — all in the name of God.

What is the answer? Put a huge, upfront emphasis on getting *every one* of your rookies (and veterans) fully trained and prepared to be successful in raising support. Set aside extensive time and money to do so *before* they are allowed to launch (or even move to) their ministry assignment. If for some reason funding dips while the staffer is doing her ministry, be willing to pull that person back for a season of additional support raising in order to return her fully funded. Yes, it might put a temporary crimp in the ministry goals, but what does this kind of training, these kinds of policies and approaches communicate to your staff? Actions speak louder than words, and it will demonstrate you want the very best for their lives. It will show you really do care!

NOTE: *Go to Chapter 11 and review how a couple of Christian organizations have done an outstanding job in giving extensive support raising training to their staff.*

45

PEOPLE IN YOUR MINISTRY WHO SHOULD <u>NOT</u> RAISE THEIR SUPPORT

Three to consider

After failing to talk a young woman out of aborting her baby, Rebecca launched a problem pregnancy ministry in a huge West Coast city. The vision started small, but 10 years later it had grown into numerous branches with more than 30 full-time workers. From the beginning, Rebecca had determined to model to her staff exactly what she was asking them to do. Consequently, Rebecca raised every penny of her personal support and trained all of her staffers to do the same. That worked fine in the early stages, but over time she became more and more frustrated because there were certain roles within the ministry for which she couldn't find (or keep) fully elf-funded staff. In addition, she started to wonder if there were also some roles that she shouldn't even *allow* them to raise their own support.

Facing these realities, Rebecca made a proposal recommending three roles she and her board would take full responsibility for funding. Here was her list and reasoning for each:

1. DEVELOPMENT OFFICER

Rebecca had brought on a gifted and motivated man to spearhead raising *major* gifts to the ministry, but he was continually torn between asking prospective donors to join his personal team (which was always in need) and giving to the organization. Rebecca put an end to his quandary, freeing him to focus *totally* on asking every single person he met to invest in the overall ministry rather than his own team. She and her board came up with a salary and expenses package that put his mind at ease and back to work fully dedicated to raising *much* bigger dollars for the organization.

2. FINANCIAL DIRECTOR

As the ministry grew the need increased for a person to do nothing but deposit, receipt, and account for the almost 2,000 gifts that came in each month. Rebecca completely trusted Lisa, the young woman who had been faithfully handling all the finances over the previous four years, but she wanted to protect Lisa from ever even being tempted to "dip into the till" because of a personal financial need. People questioned why Rebecca included Lisa in this list of "Organizationally Funded Staff" because there had never been a hint of financial impropriety, and besides, Lisa was at full support. Rebecca acknowledged those points but pressed ahead, crafting a generous salary that would cover all of Lisa's needs. As the leader, Rebecca was not willing to risk the ministry's reputation for financial integrity she had worked so hard to establish over the years with even one slip up.

3. SECRETARY

It seemed like they could never get someone in this role who could raise a healthy and consistent team of givers. Rebecca would get them trained, started, and functioning in their ministry assignments, but it was just a matter of time until low support caused the secretary to cut back or drop out altogether. The ministry desperately needed someone year-in and year-out in this critical administrative role. Rebecca resolved to find the very best person she could and pay what that person was worth in order to ensure the long-term continuity and excellence she knew the ministry needed to sustain growth.

Rebecca requested that all three of these people ask their supporters to continue to give monthly to the organization's general fund, because now *that* fund would pay their salaries. She included a note in their next month's receipts, and then all three staffers followed up with phone calls to see if the donors had received the note, understood it, and would be open to continuing to invest.

NOTE: *There may be others in your organization that for one reason or another you want to (or need to) pay them rather than require them to raise their support. Also, as I mentioned before, there may be a valid reason for the CEO to take his or her salary out of the major donations they raise. My personal preference, though? The three listed above.*

46

ADMINISTRATIVE STAFF

Getting them fully funded

A reporter asked the same question to three bricklayers who were busy constructing a huge cathedral: "What are you doing?" The first worker smirked, "I'm laying bricks." The second smiled and said, "I'm building a church." But the third stood up, raised his hands to the sky and proclaimed, "I am bringing glory to God!"

All three men were doing the exact same thing, but with radically different perspectives. Similarly, I have talked to many administrative staff over the years whose job titles may be the same, but are worlds apart in how they view their roles:

- "I just type and talk on the phone all day."
- "I provide administrative support for all our staff."
- "I am the vital link between our missionaries on the field and our home office as we seek to plant 10,000 churches among the unreached by the year 2020."

Three different administrators were doing the exact same things, but they had radically different perspectives. Even though these administrative staffers are worth their weight in gold and absolutely essential to the success of the ministry, many leaders don't value them like we should. Consequently, they don't put much stock in themselves and when they look a potential donor in the eye, it is hard for them to truly believe their role is really that critical.

So, how can we help these administrative staff members view themselves as a great investment to potential donors who may normally give to the seemingly more "strategic" or "frontline" worker rather than the behind-the-scenes office staff?

1. PRIZE THEM

As they begin to raise support, don't give them a job title like "assistant," but something with vision like "Director of Ministry Advancement." Continually include them in the big picture discussions and decisions.

2. PRAISE THEM

Make heroes out of them. One of the greatest human needs is appreciation. If you continually (publicly and privately) affirm them, they will want to be part of the team, want to get to full support, want to make a long-term commitment.

3. PREPARE THEM

Give them great support-raising training and materials. Make sure their newsletters are full of changed lives, from their own personal ministries, yes, but also showing fruit from the ministry they provide the administrative foundation and stability to. Help them see it's not just about typing letters or answering calls, it is about serving the greater cause of world evangelization.

I've read that for every U.S. soldier we have on the front lines, we have eight support personnel someplace making sure they have everything they need. I am hoping your field staff to administration ratio is not that high, but whatever it is, make sure you focus your administration staff on the vision of the ministry, and not just their particular tasks.

47

CONNECTING YOU TO MAJOR DONORS

How staff members can be the bridge

Here's the scene: Stella Staffer has raised her monthly support, reported to her ministry assignment, and is off to a good start.

She also is faithfully staying connected to her financial partners through newsletters, periodic phone calls, and visits. In the process, Marla and Major Donor, one of the couples who support her, express their desire to learn more about the organization's vision and leadership, and she is glad to share.

But panic strikes Stella one day when she finds out the president of the ministry is coming through town trying to raise some major gifts for the whole organization. She doesn't want her donor couple to meet the president because they might decide to give their $300 a month to the organization rather than to her. So she hems and haws, telling the ministry leaders she can't really think of anybody who might be a candidate to give larger gifts. In fact, word has spread through the grapevine, and all of the ministry's staff members from town-to-town are protecting their potential bigger givers from the "greedy claws" of the organization's development officers.

The problem: Stella and her co-workers have it all backward. When staff members identify someone on their teams who is (or could be) a large donor, they should instead work hard to *introduce* that giver to the leadership of the ministry. Studies show that when a person gives to an individual *and* the organization, commitment, loyalty, and longevity increase significantly — to both parties. When staff members catch this spirit of sharing (vs. hoarding) supporters, it opens up entire new networks of potential givers to the ministry. This results in a healthier organization that trickles down to a healthier staff and programs.

Wise staff members cheerfully share their supporters with ministry leadership.

FOUR TRUTHS

- Givers like Marla and Major Donor probably won't write Stella a $50,000 check for her personal support.

- If they can meet the ministry leaders and grasp the organization's vision — and are asked to invest — they might just write that check.

- This initiates a triangle of trust between the givers, the staff person, and the leadership, where everyone wins — not to mention the brownie points the staffer obtains in the process.

- Our supporters don't belong to us (or the organization). They belong to God, and He has temporarily shared them with us. If we're not willing to share them with others, He might just take them away from us.

48

THE SUPPORT-RAISING DNA OF YOUR ORGANIZATION

How to re-create it

Marv was a dynamic 41-year-old visionary who took the challenge of a lifetime when he left a young, vibrant mission agency to take the helm of a larger, decades-old ministry stuck in the past. As he got to know the staff during the first few months, he jotted down a number of unhealthy attitudes and issues he sensed had formed and hardened over the years. He was tempted to pull out a jackhammer, break it all apart, and start over, but instead he wisely took a took a deep breath, bowed, and prayed, "Oh God, only You can re-create the DNA of this organization. Please give me grace, wisdom, and perseverance."

His list?

- Ministry leaders were taking privileges and perks the other staff could not.
- Executives were paid salaries and not required to raise their support.
- There were too many administrators in ratio to field staff.
- Some staff were subsidized while others were not.
- There was no solid support training or policies in place.
- A "poverty mentality" had developed among the staff to cover their unwillingness to raise their full support.
- A fear of personal evangelism lent itself toward adopting a "don't ask" approach to support raising. Leaders older than him were suspicious and resistant.
- Staff recruiting was down and new candidates were not strong leaders.

No wonder morale was low, trust was non-existent, and organizational and staff finances were at rock bottom. So, Marv, his wife, and a kindred-spirit board member prayed and listed six steps they would implement:

1. SPEND THE FIRST YEAR WATCHING AND LISTENING

Marv interviewed past and present board members, executives, staff members, spouses, major donors, and key ministry partners, asking what they saw as the ministry's support raising "Strengths, Weaknesses, Opportunities, and Threats." He also resolved to never "over respond" to some of the staff's whining, grumbling, and small thinking.

2. BE A CONSISTENT MODEL

He made no big changes the first year, but mainly prayed, loved, and served. Marv and his wife worked to turn the organizational chart upside down, asking God to use their life and sacrifice to melt the rebellion and apathy around them. They made sure their own personal monthly support team was healthy and consistent.

3. GET THE STAFF IN THE WORD

He gathered the staff each week for a time of prayer and study of the Scriptures. He (and others) chose passages on vision, passion, faith, courage, evangelism, giving, asking, and examples of living on support. The Holy Spirit began to work in people's hearts.

4. WIN OVER THE KEY LEADERS

Along with spending extensive time with new staff members who hadn't been "infected" by poor attitudes, Marv identified four veterans he deemed key influencers. He encouraged, listened, and brainstormed with them as they helped him craft support-raising policies, practices, and reporting. Because Marv valued them enough to truly let them "weigh in," they began to "buy in" to his leadership and new paradigms he was introducing.

5. SECURE THE BEST TRAINING POSSIBLE

Marv and his team researched the various training options and determined they would pay any price in time and money to get their staff the very best training available. This communicated how critical being at full support was, that the leadership cared about their marriages and families, and how interested they were in the ministry longevity of each staffer.

6. DO WHAT IS NECESSARY

One supporter had actually counseled Marv to just walk away and start his own ministry, joking, "It's easier to give birth than raise the dead!" But Marv felt God's call to stay for the long haul, knowing if the Lord was going to "re-create" the support-raising DNA of the organization, it would mean surrendering his rights and embracing the heart and mind of Jesus. He printed a card for his desk that read: "A servant-leader is someone who *does what is necessary* ... "

Marv decided not to put a period at the end of that sentence.

Section VIII

More Viewpoints:
Nine 'Second Opinions' to Assess

49

WITH MANY COUNSELORS THERE IS VICTORY

BY MATTHEW PACE

I have fond memories of my twelve-month mission effort reaching out to college students in India. The ministry there was pure joy, but as my year wound down I battled a nagging question: "What am I going to do now?" I had three great options on the table with three outstanding organizations, but only about a month left to decide which I should choose. The main thought running through my head was: "I need some help!!" Of course I had been praying about it for a while, but there was no voice from heaven commanding me where to go. The more I thought about it, the more I realized I would be wise to tap into a ready-made source of help God had already provided for me — my supporters!

So I wrote an email to them explaining my options and asking for prayer and advice. The response was amazing. All kinds of people contacted me, sharing their hearts and thoughts. Some gave counsel in areas I had not considered and started their correspondence with, "Have you thought about … ?" Some wrote back specifically telling me why I would be great in a *particular* ministry role. A host of supporters agreed it was a difficult choice and that all three options seemed appealing. Most of all, everyone who responded said, "I will be praying for this decision."

Just from writing this one short email I received new perspective, personal encouragement and affirmation, and a reinvigorated team of prayer warriors coming before God asking for wisdom. When I finally made my decision, I wrote a letter back to my supporters explaining what route I had chosen and why. And their response? They wrote back with reassurances they had been praying for me and were excited about my new direction. By far, the majority of them stayed on my support team and are still investing in me today. They had bought in!!

When I think about all the great folks who support me, I picture a team. I'm playing one role and them another. I can't accomplish this ministry without a team, and when you don't let your team "weigh in" on your major decisions, it's foolish — even selfish. My encouragement to you? Determine to be a team player by letting your supporters weigh in *before* expecting them to buy in!

Matt Pace is a [well-supported!] staff member of Student Mobilization at the University of Central Arkansas. His campus ministry is described in the chapter "One Spiritual Arsonist I Want You To Meet" in the book Brown Like Coffee.

PREPARING TO ASK BIG

BY SHARON EPPS

O ne of the best biblical examples of "a big ask" is tucked away in the story of Jesus' triumphal entry told in Matthew 21. As Jesus and the disciples approached Jerusalem, He sent two disciples ahead. *"'Go into the village over there,' he said, 'and you will see a donkey tied there, with its colt beside it. Untie them and bring them here. If anyone asks what you are doing, just say, "The Lord needs them," and he will immediately send them.'"* (Matthew 21:2-3, NLT)

Can you imagine what the owner of the animals might have thought as the disciples started walking away with his only source of transportation and most likely his livelihood? It would be similar to someone driving away in your car and taking your computer, too! Scripture doesn't record the owner's response, but it appears he willingly donated the animals. How could that be? When faithful servants understand that the Master wants to put their treasure to use, they celebrate the opportunity to participate.

My task in support raising includes the responsibility to walk with the donor in understanding:

- God owns everything.
- The reality that Kingdom investments yield eternal results.
- My willingness to be held accountable to manage their investment faithfully.

As I prepare to "ask big," I must assess my faithfulness with that which God has already provided me. Am I personally faithful as a manager of God's resources — finances, relationships, skills, talents, and use of time? Luke 16:10 says, *"Whoever can be trusted with very little can also be trusted with much."*

Asking big could offend if I haven't been a trustworthy manager. If, however, I have faithfully cultivated the relationship, ensuring that the truths of God's ownership, eternal Kingdom investments, and my willing accountability are embraced, the donor often celebrates the opportunity to participate at a significant level.

Sharon Epps is a consultant and speaker for Woman Doing Well. She helps churches and individuals energize stewardship and generosity through her firm, Kinetic Consultants, as well as incubating innovative ways to reach next gen women through Freestyle Living, Inc. She lives in Georgia with her husband and four children.

51

PURGING 'POOR TALK' FROM YOUR MOUTH AND HEART

BY HENRI MOREAU

Two years ago I desperately wanted a laptop computer. One day I was visiting a supporter named Mark, and he had just purchased the fastest machine on the market. I salivated after seeing it and found myself subconsciously wishing I had money to purchase one. Deep down, I also knew he could afford to buy me one. As thoughts like, *"If I weren't a missionary, I'd be able to buy something like that"* raced through my mind I suddenly blurted out, "Mark, it must be nice to be able to afford a computer like that. I could really use one of those."

It was A-plus poor talk. Immediately the Holy Spirit spoke to my heart, *"Henri, you are such a manipulator!"* I felt ashamed and began a journey to remove poor talk from my life. What is the cure? For one, you must get to 100 percent of your budget to fully support your family and provide for all the ministry needs you encounter — even for computers. As God supplies, you will see his love and grace for you.

Next, budget enough money to be a generous giver to those you're ministering to. As a campus missionary, I modeled to my students how God was an awesome provider. I took numerous students out for meals each week, never letting them pay. When they asked how I could afford this on a "missionary" budget, I told them, *"Are you kidding? God has provided so much for me I can't even spend it all!"* Not only did it feel good to bless our students, but my excitement about God's provision rubbed off on them. After adopting this attitude and lifestyle, I began seeing a number of students say yes to the call of ministry. They saw God provide for me and that gave them the confidence to trust Him for their future too.

Last, seek ways to minister to your support team. For me, this took the form of special cards and small gifts to remind them how much I appreciated them. I found that when I concentrated on "how I could give to them," my temptation to "poor talk" or to try to "get something from them" declined.

Poor talk? Never again!

Henri Moreau ministered on campuses in California with Chi Alpha for 15 years before becoming the organization's national support-raising specialist. Ironically, he began his ministry in 1991, two years after running away from God's call because he was afraid of raising support.

52

HOW TO GO BACK TO LONG-LOST FRIENDS

BY DALE LOSCH

Most of us who raise personal support have an inordinate fear of offending people if we ask them to consider becoming a financial partner. This fear is accentuated even more if the person is someone with whom we haven't had contact for many years. *Inordinate* means *"not within reasonable bounds,"* and it's an apt description of such fear. I know. I've been there.

After attending The Support Raising Solutions training, I committed myself to applying the principles of personally asking people to consider becoming financial partners. I prayerfully compiled a list of all the acquaintances, past and present, whom I believed God would have us contact. Many of these were people we hadn't seen for years. It's amazing how "creative" our minds can get when it comes to rationalizing why we shouldn't contact a given person. For virtually everyone on my list, I had at least one "good" reason why I shouldn't ask him to consider joining our team, the foremost of which was my lack of any meaningful contact with the person over a long period of time.

I swallowed my fears and forged ahead with the plan. I contacted a former youth sponsor from the first church I served in as a 21-year-old Bible college graduate, a wealthy businessman with whom I had only a passing acquaintance, and a member of a small group I had once led. How would they respond to my rather unexpected contact?

My fears were indeed *inordinate* — far outside of reasonable bounds. I was amazed that out of the 30 people I contacted, not a single one seemed offended. Rather I was usually met with a spectrum of emotions that ranged from sympathetic to exuberant. The former youth sponsor invited us for dinner and happily joined our team. The businessman who we hardly knew gave us the largest monthly commitment we've ever received in the 20 years since we began our missionary career. The former small group member marveled at the perfect timing of our contact, and said he believed God was in it.

So, an honest, tastefully written letter of introduction, followed by a phone call and a personal visit turned inordinate fears into extraordinary fruit. Over half of those we contacted joined our support team, and many old friendships were rekindled. Nothing was lost and much was gained.

Dale Losch is the President of CrossWorld, a missionary sending organization committed to making disciples and establishing local fellowships where few exist. Dale, his wife Jerusha, and their four children live in Mississauga, Canada.

53

FROM BUSINESSMAN TO SUPPORT RAISER

BY BILL GLIDDEN

A full year after I was accepted onto the staff of American Missionary Fellowship, I found myself continually asking, "How am I ever going to come up with the time to talk to people face to face about this ministry?" Owning a small business meant spending all day with customers and evenings doing paperwork. With only bits of time in between, it seemed it would take years to get 100 percent funded.

Seeking God's direction, I was hearing and seeing nothing. Then we were asked to go to an SRS Bootcamp. I didn't feel I needed more training, and I certainly didn't need to lose three days of work. At the SRS Bootcamp, though, we learned asking is biblical and how we view God and ministry will determine our success in support raising. When the trainer challenged us to raise support *full-time*, I knew this was why I was here and this was God's will.

So another new adventure with God began, and I could see how He had prepared me to take this huge step of faith. We thought of people who could support us for a three-month window, allowing us to raise support full-time. Five people committed to launching us. Two actually *asked* if they could be supporters! The other three were very busy people, but still I shared with them the vision God had given us and how they could help. I gave them a proposal of our plans and goals for the three months of support raising and the move to our ministry assignment.

Now that I was free to raise support full-time, I had the flexibility to fit into the schedules of the people I asked for appointments. At one point, I was making a lot of calls but not getting many appointments. I prayed and was reminded of those who weren't on our list and who

I hadn't thought of calling. The first name on my new list became a $200 monthly supporter!

Meeting people over meals or in their homes allowed them to get to know me and the AMF mission better. We were able to share the passion God had given us and ask them to partner with us financially. Who said support raising is drudgery? I had the privilege of meeting new people, renewing old relationships, talking about Jesus, and sharing the excitement of this new ministry. That's hard to beat!

Bill Glidden was self-employed for more than 20 years. After he and his wife Mary felt the call to join AMF and were shown how to go full-time raising support, they put their team together and moved to Walsenburg, Colorado as missionaries.

THE HEART TRANSFORMATION OF A SUPPORT RAISER'S WIFE

BY PAM NOLEN

Have you ever received an envelope of cash in the mail without a note or return address? Or been sent a check that equaled what you just spent on a big-ticket item? These events, and more, happened to us, and it was a revolutionary time in my life.

My husband and I had been on staff with a campus ministry for five years, and I had not enjoyed the support-raising aspect at all. I knew when we were engaged I was marrying a man fully devoted to ministry for the rest of our lives. I just didn't realize it would take five years for me to move from the "ought to" to the "want to" attitude of living on support.

We were living on partially raised support along with my teaching salary. When our first child arrived, we took a huge step of faith by me transitioning to a stay-at-home mom and us living totally on support. This is when my heavenly Father changed my heart. We saw the Lord provide at every turn, and many times in miraculous ways. I finally realized the Lord is going to take care of us! It sounds so simple and yet this was when I grasped how living on support gives us continuous opportunities to trust Him completely with all our needs (Matthew 6:25-34).

With a new outlook on support raising, I began to embrace living as a wife of a support raiser. I began praying more for our supporters, writing postcards, and partnering with my husband in this aspect of our lives. We did reach full support, which brought a healthier budget and us making wiser decisions on everyday spending and long-term savings. This shift was a mile-marker for us and produced a stronger marriage.

I share this with hopes of impacting a spouse toward embracing how exciting life can be living on support: It nurtures a lifestyle of trusting our Father and gives you "living by faith" stories to share with others. It also provides a built-in method for communicating with those whom God places in your life as supporters.

As we transitioned from campus ministry to a church staff one year ago, I was asked if it would be a relief to not have to live on support any longer. My immediate response was no, I truly enjoyed the life of a support-raising spouse.

Pam Nolen lives with her husband Clark and their three boys in Fayetteville, Arkansas. Even though Clark is on staff with Northwest Arkansas Fellowship Bible Church and draws a salary, she truly misses living on support and all the."benefits" it affords! Pam radiates a love for Christ, family, friends, and the college girls she disciples. She also enjoys cycling and antiquing.

55

SPIRITUAL WARFARE AND SUPPORT RAISING

BY JOHN MAISEL

R aising support creates the same tension and conflict that believers often face when presenting the Gospel. Christians usually can stay focused when they understand spiritual warfare is involved in asking someone to trust Christ. We need to recognize the same battle exists when we ask others to financially give toward the Great Commission. Satan shoots big darts of deception at our minds. We all need to strive toward trusting God rather than worrying about what someone may or may not think about our request for money. This will help us stay focused.

This, of course, is easier said than done. When I ask someone to consider giving to my support team, it is tempting to feel like I am trespassing private boundaries regarding a person's financial status with my personal needs for his or her money. However, I must immediately ask myself, "Is this for my glory or for God's glory?"

The answer infuses me with courage.

Ministry is a faith-filled path with lessons to learn and instruction to teach us dependence on our Redeemer. Just as Satan never wants you to ask a person if he or she would like to pray to receive Christ, so the "father of lies" never wants you to ask people to support you in your work of sharing the love of Christ. When we understand this, we are less likely to cut and run.

Recently, I asked a donor who historically had given $25,000 a year to the organization to consider a three-year commitment of $50,000 for each year. He agreed to continue the $25,000. I asked him to pray about it for one week, and he promised he would. After a week, he called and told me he had prayed and then said, "God convicted me to give $100,000 per year over the next three years!"

My friend, God is at work and delights to use our circumstances to prove His power. We must stand against our enemy and resist the temptation to flee.

John Maisel is the founder of East West Ministries, which focuses on evangelism and church planting in areas where the Gospel is virtually non-existent. John and his wife, Susie, live in Dallas. They have one daughter and two grandchildren.

56

GIVE BEFORE YOU ASK

BY JEFF ANDERSON

Support raisers must be givers. I consider personal generosity among the most important factors to successful fund-raising. If God blesses givers, then support raisers can't afford to miss God's blessings from their own funding efforts.

I've been raising support for six years, and I'm continually humbled by God's call for me into ministry and to raising support. One thing I have learned is I cannot ask donors to do what I myself do not do. If I don't even give to my local church, how could I possibly ask donors to give beyond their local churches to support my ministry? If I do not personally support another missionary or para-church organization, how then can I relate to those I engage for funding? And if I've never taken the step of faith to commit a "break-out" gift (sacrificial or special gift) in my personal giving journey, then how can I ask someone else to make a similar gift to my ministry?

In a sense, my personal giving serves as a ceiling for the measure of gift I can ask of others. The more I give and experience the joy of giving, the greater my funnel of opportunity for lifting the generosity in others. I call this "earning the right to ask." It is hypocritical to engage in this spiritual activity of asking unless we have first *fully* participated in the spiritual activity of giving. While we don't earn this right by advertising our giving to others (that would violate scripture), a growing, personal giving journey does provide a sense of confidence, courage, and conviction that helps us approach prospective givers. We will experience a clear conscience, a freedom, an empowering to make the "big ask" of donors, inspiring them to invest even greater amounts. For some reason, making the "big ask" comes easier after I have made the "big give!"

When I entered the ministry six years ago, my family adjusted to a significantly lower salary, yet we did not compromise our high standard of giving. As a result, God's blessings have been abundant and have positioned me with the confidence and integrity to engage other givers. Personal giving growth can help support raisers overcome the fear of asking. Everyone needs to experience the generosity journey. Maybe your donors just need a ministry leader to lift them. Be that ministry leader. Give first, and then ask.

Jeff Anderson lives in Tulsa, Oklahoma, with his wife Stephanie and four children. He is the author of Plastic Donuts and serves as the Founder and President for Acceptable Gift Inc.

57

FORTY YEARS OF SUPPORT RAISING

BY DR. ART DEYO

I have trained hundeds of young people to raise their support for their calling into youth ministry over the last forty years. Sadly, some don't make it because of the attitude of their parents. Many don't even apply because their parents say, "You need to get a real job!" Just today, I talked with a youth pastor who, along with his wife and children, feel called to Germany as missionaries. But his parents are reluctant and her parents strongly oppose their going, partly because of support raising. He wanted to know how to respond to them.

I told him first to be sure of their call. Second, he and his wife need to grieve with their parents because it will definitely be a loss for both parents and children to be so far away from each other. Third, I assured him that where the Lord guides, He also provides. If God is in it, who can be against it?

Over the years I have seen thousands of people respond positively by giving to a young person who has been called by God into Christian ministry. Support raising is not begging. It is giving people an opportunity to make an eternal investment that will beat anything the stock market does — hands-down! And there is no substitute for the caring and praying these giving partners will do.

My wife and I have raised support for forty years in Youth For Christ. Never have we gone without a paycheck. God has provided all the way through. Our daughter and son-in-law are in youth ministry, too, and have raised support for 15 years. Now they have to triple what they raise to go to Europe as missionaries.

Though we will miss them and our two grandsons when they move to Europe, we are so proud of them for following the Lord. We are doing all we can to encourage them in their support-raising efforts. We wouldn't have it any other way! It is my prayer that you will welcome the calling the Lord has placed on your sons or daughters and that you will encourage them and support them in all they have to do to prepare for their upcoming ministry. More than anything else, it is a real job. In fact, helping people find Christ could be the most fulfilling job a person could ever have.

Dr. Art Deyo is the former director of missionary development for Youth For Christ/USA in Englewood, Colorado. He and his wife Lois have been on support and served with YFC for forty-two years in various leadership roles around the U.S. and world.

Section IX

Eight Bonus Features to Peruse

58

THE TOP FOUR BOOKS
ON SUPPORT RAISING

- *Friend Raising: Building a Missionary Support Team that Lasts,* by Betty Barnett (YWAM, 1991)
  Barnett is on staff with Youth With A Mission and trains missionary staff around the world. In her short but powerful book, she teaches the four practical pillars of lasting friend and support raising: Friend-Raising, Generosity, Communication, and Prayer with Promises. She brings a warm and enduring emphasis on building lifelong relationships with our supporters. Barnett exudes a genuine authenticity through her own story and the testimonies of Christian workers who have succeeded (and struggled) to apply her training.

- *Funding Your Ministry: Whether You're Gifted or Not,* by Scott Morton (Dawson Media, 1999; revised 2007)
  Morton, vice president of development for The Navigators, oversees major fund development and training for staff to raise their support. True to The Navigators, the book is based on a thorough study of the Scriptures. Easy to read and full of great cartoons and practical tools, Morton makes this sometimes fearful topic less intimidating. The Bible studies and exercises in the appendix should be required homework for every person raising support. Having lived on personal support for almost 40 years, Morton walks the talk.

- *Getting Sent: A Relational Approach to Support Raising,* by Pete Sommer (InterVarsity Press, 1999)
  Sommer has been on and off the staff of IVCF for years, ministering on various campuses and training staff how to raise support. In his insightful book, he identifies with the obstacles and struggles we all face when he writes, "Most of us would rather have a root canal than ask for money!" The book

includes nine Bible studies that show the principles undergirding Sommer's approach. Focused on getting to know the people you ask for support, he has helpful sections that address the unique challenges that women, minorities, and different ethnic groups might face in raising support.

- *People Raising: A Practical Guide to Raising Support,* by Bill Dillon (Moody Press, 1993)
  Dillon, the executive director of Inner City Impact in Chicago, trains his staff and others in raising their support. Probably the most widely read of the four books, Dillon helps the reader cultivate positive attitudes and skills necessary for successful support raising. He includes insightful quotes from leaders, step-by-step phone and presentation scripts, sample letters, forms to record information, and training exercises. Over the last 20-plus years, God has used Dillon to disseminate basic support-raising principles to thousands.

NOTE: *This list of books is in no particular order. All four are excellent and make unique contributions to the healthy and overall training of Christian workers to raise their support.*

59

FIVE CURRENT TRENDS IN PERSONAL SUPPORT RAISING

NOTE: *This chapter reinforces (some would say repeats!) what you have read in other chapters of this book. This synthesizing of various trends may be helpful to you or others to get a snapshot of the current state of support raising among Christian ministries in the U.S.*

1. MINISTRIES APPROACH SUPPORT RAISING JUST LIKE THEY APPROACH WITNESSING

Those who aren't willing or able to ask people to receive Christ in their personal ministry usually aren't willing or able to ask people to give during their support-raising appointments. We may blame our support failures on lack of contacts, lack of experience, etc., but maybe that's just a smokescreen to hide our fears. The groups that have broken through the faith (and fear) barriers of consistently doing personal evangelism not only attract more staff, but also usually get them to full support much quicker.

2. VERY FEW MINISTRIES ENFORCE THE 100 PERCENT POLICY

Many ministries have the "can't report to your assignment until you're at 100 percent" policy, but few have the courage or consistency to enforce it — for everyone, *no exceptions*. Plus, if the leaders of the ministry are on paid salaries they don't have a lot of credibility or authority to enforce it. I don't allow our new staff to even move to their new ministry location until they have 100 percent of their monthly support coming in, not just pledged. It may seem cruel, but you will be doing your staff a huge favor, and you'll see remarkable results.

3. THE "DON'T ASK" GROUPS ARE MOVING TOWARD AN "ASKING IS OK" STANCE

Some of the old-line mission agencies created in the wake of Hudson Taylor's ministry have been struggling attracting staff, getting them funded, and getting them to the field in a timely manner. Many are becoming open to sharing their financial need and asking in a sensitive way. Taylor is a great role model in many areas, but his funding approach may not be the best in this time and culture. Why is it OK to ask people to pray (which many of these groups do), but not ask them to give? Sure seems confusing and contradictory that some groups have separated those two and implied that one is good and the other is bad.

4. MINISTRIES ARE STARTING TO GIVE MORE EMPHASIS TO SUPPORT-RAISING TRAINING

Many Christian ministries give a two-hour "orientation" on support raising, or worse, just hand the new staffer a book to read. There is a move to give one or two days, or more, to this important area. Along with creating new policies and tools, some groups are appointing and equipping someone within their organization to train and track their staff full-time. Our ministry is trying to provide the training and curriculum for these smaller and mid-size ministries to do quality training in-house, for their own staff. You can go to the Resources section to see what is involved for one of your staff to become an SRS Certified Trainer.

5. MINISTRIES REALLY DON'T HAVE A FEEL FOR THE SUPPORT-RAISING HEALTH OF THEIR ORGANIZATIONS

It's a fog out there. Leaders hope their staff members are doing OK in their support, finances, debt load, marriages, savings, giving, and communication with supporters. But, they have no concrete evidence to tell them one way or the other. Our Support Raising Solutions Ministry Audit objectively and anonymously surveys the staff, evaluates the results, and makes recommendations for change. The organizations willing to take a hard look at themselves and make the necessary adjustments make the greatest long-term impact.

NOTE: *Again, these suggested policies are a recap of so much we have already discussed, but I thought it might be helpful to have the bare essentials boiled down and listed here.*

60

FIVE IRONCLAD POLICIES
EVERY MINISTRY SHOULD HAVE

I saw the value of "tough love" while raising three sons. When they were growing up, creating firm family policies gave us a sense of direction, stability, even protection. I've got a long way to go in leading our family and ministry, but I have experienced the benefit of forming (and sticking to) some basic practices that help everyone succeed.

Most ministries don't create this brand of organizational DNA at their founding. I have seen a few groups attempt to "re-create" their DNA after struggling for years, but there is a price to pay. As a leader in your ministry, you must possess a total "buy in." Why? Because your commitment and follow-through must be ironclad: "so firm, so secure, as to be unbreakable."

For para-church ministries that require staff to raise their personal support, I suggest these policies that can help produce the unity and longevity you yearn to see in your staff:

1. LEADERS MUST RAISE SUPPORT

Yes, the leadership raises organizational funds, but this is different. Credibility and authority (to even create and enforce these policies) can be increased if the leaders are willing to start from scratch and put together 100 percent of their own *personal, monthly* support. This may or may not be possible, but do all you can to strive toward this. **Result:** Morale

2. PROVIDE THOROUGH PREPARATION AND TRAINING

You'll do ministry *just* like you raise support. You raise support just like you *prepare* to raise support. You prepare to raise support the way you were *trained*. You'll never regret spending extensive time and money getting *everyone* on your staff the best possible training. **Result:** Excellence

3. REQUIRE STRONG ACCOUNTABILITY EVERY WEEK

During the support-raising time, make sure *every* staff member has a very detailed accountability partner he/she reports to *every* week — like Monday morning. Require the support raiser to fill out a standardized document that lists weekly goals and measurable results. (Hint: An accountability partner with some spine has a way of strengthening our backbone, too!) **Result:** Teamwork

4. INSIST ON 100 PERCENT SUPPORT BEFORE REPORTING TO ASSIGNMENT

You'll be doing your staff members a huge favor by *not* letting them start their ministry, or even *move* to their assignment, until they have reached *at least* 100 percent of their budget — not pledges or one-time gifts, but *monthly* checks (or EFT forms) in hand. Fudging on this removes all the (healthy) pressure the staff and donors feel to quickly get to full support. **Result:** Urgency

5. CONNECT WITH SUPPORTERS AT LEAST BI-MONTHLY

Every other month is not too often to require your staff members to thank and communicate with their ministry partners. A call, a note, or a newsletter at least every 60 days tells those supporters you care about them and value their investment in you. **Result:** Gratitude

If you choose to implement "ironclad" policies like these, I believe you'll see dramatic results in your staff, their marriages, job performance, and support. Take the long look and don't cut corners. Tough love. It can sometimes be the very best kind.

61

A SUPPORT-RAISING SURVEY OF 100 SENDING AGENCIES

Maybe you ran into one of the women from our dedicated staff at one of the last few Urbana Missions Conferences in St. Louis. Representatives from The Center for Mission Mobilization spent several days diligently surveying people from the more than 100 different mission agencies with exhibits there. Just as the ministry leaders they questioned didn't claim to have *total* knowledge, we aren't presenting ourselves as "research scholars." We're simply trying to come up with some "pretty close" figures as to how Christian workers are doing in support raising. The survey included three basic questions:

1. WHAT PERCENTAGE OF YOUR STAFF WOULD YOU ESTIMATE TO BE AT 100 PERCENT SUPPORT?

Only 48 percent — less than half of all the people on staff with these organizations — are at full support. That's the discouraging news. The encouraging part is that 16 out of the

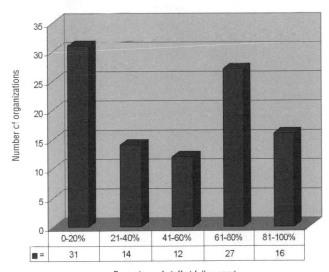

	0-20%	21-40%	41-60%	61-80%	81-100%
■ =	31	14	12	27	16

Percentage of staff at full support

100 organizations had 81-100 percent of their staff at full support. So, it can happen. Plus, based on extensive follow-up conversations, our staff concluded that low support levels probably are *not* due to an inability to raise support, but are linked more to organizational policies, expectations, and training.

2. HOW LONG DO YOU ESTIMATE IT TAKES YOUR AVERAGE STAFF MEMBER TO RAISE FULL SUPPORT?

The average estimated time it takes a staff member to raise full support is 17 months. A number of external factors need to be taken into consideration, such as the amount of support the staffer needed to raise and whether the staff member was raising support full- or part-time. This 17-month figure encouraged us. At the 2003 Urbana conference, we did a similar survey, and the average length of time to get to full support was 23 months. So, maybe we are making progress!

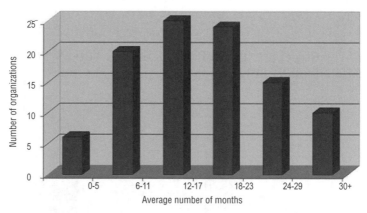

3. HOW MUCH TIME DOES YOUR ORGANIZATION ALLOT TO SUPPORT-RAISING TRAINING?

The time organizations spend on support-raising training was all over the board. Some, we sensed, did not offer any training in this area at all, but were reluctant to admit that.

On the other hand (as hard as it is for me to believe), five different groups said they spent 10 days training staff on how to raise support. Please, if you spend more than six full days in support training, let me know. I have a gold star I want to give you!

Last, the groups with 0-7 hours of training had significanly fewer staff members at 100 percent support, indicating that traing plays a critical role in the success of support-raising efforts.

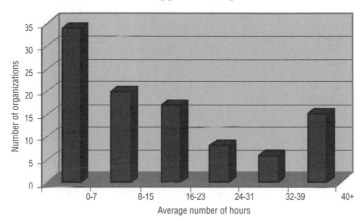

62

THREE SECRETS TO SAVE YOUR CEO FROM A HEART ATTACK!

B axter was a fun-loving visionary who attracted all kinds of sharp and gifted people to him and his ministry. He not only made them feel like they had a unique contribution to make, but also that they would forever be his best friend.

Early on, Baxter decided to draw upon his vast number of successful business friends to fund all his organizations' needs. This allowed him to recruit impressive staff and develop exciting programs. After about ten years, however, he suddenly hit "the wall." Marathoners know full well the sinking feeling of being halfway through the race when a bomb explodes inside their bodies, instantly robbing them of every ounce of energy or willpower to go on. Baxter's "wall" came in the form of a heart attack.

Similarly, the leader in your ministry has a limit on how many staff he can recruit, how many "big hitters" he can cultivate, how many fires he can put out, how many plane trips, board meetings, and speaking engagements he can handle. Something's got to give when a leader tries to meet everyone's expectations (including family) by constantly keeping an unrealistic number of balls in the air. Here are three secrets to help your leader stay healthy:

1. PERSONAL SUPPORT: BE A "DOWN AND OUTER"

All ministries choose (or fall into) either a centralized or decentralized philosophy of funding their staff. If the leader makes the (sometimes fatal) decision to raise *all* the staff salaries, she may want to go ahead and make reservations at the local ER. But, pushing the responsibility "down and out" by requiring staff members to raise *all* their own support, through their *own* personal contacts, will ultimately involve many more givers who can provide a multitude of new funding sources.

2. PROGRAM EXPENSES: GET BIG BY THINKING SMALL

Break down the organization into units or teams. Help the leader of each department or region to go beyond just raising her own support to where he also embraces the responsibility of recruiting all the staff and funds to keep that area strong and growing. There may be resistance at first if this is a new concept, but this decentralized philosophy has a way of weeding out the weak links in an organization and attracting (and developing) stronger, more visionary staff. The whole is always a sum of its parts, and ultimately the overall ministry will thrive by having an ever-broadening network of leaders who are shouldering the financial burdens.

3. THE HUMAN FACTOR: THEY DESERVE A BREAK TODAY

Staff members who have taken on the load of raising their own personal support *and* their program expenses take some of the pressure off the CEO. You would be doing your leader (and your ministry) a huge favor by making sure he has plenty of regular opportunities to get away and pray, plan, and recharge. This not only allows time to do long-range planning and preparation, but also contributes toward a strong spiritual, emotional, and, yes, even physical health.

63

SUCCESSFUL SUPPORT RAISING IN A SUFFERING ECONOMY

What's a support-raising Christian worker to do when things get *so* bad it's more appropriate to spell it *ickonomy* rather than *economy*? Should you do the "security shuffle," scrambling to interview for church staff or secular positions? Afraid not. They're slashing budgets and employees, too. Yes, some of your donors' 401Ks turned into 201Ks overnight, but God is still in control, and clinging to the six pillars I list below may help you weather the financial tornadoes intent upon wreaking havoc on the economy — and our support teams.

1. REVIEW YOUR CALLING

Go back and remember when and how God led you into this ministry and reaffirm that conviction. When you get to heaven someday and review the tapes of your life, the Lord may ask, "Do you want to view the good times first or the bad?" Guess what? From God's perspective, these tumultuous, faith-stretching experiences may be part of the "Good Times Highlight Reel."

2. DON'T PANIC

Do not send out crisis letters. People might respond once, but if you ever do it again they'll conclude: "Either this Christian worker doesn't know how to manage his money or he needs to raise more support." Ron Frey, veteran fundraiser, asks, "Can we count on the resiliency of our economy or the good will of the American people to support our causes?" My answer is a resounding NO! Even though the nightly news feeds peoples' fear by likening our situation to The Great Depression 2, our security is in God and God alone!

3. DIVERSIFY YOUR MINISTRY PARTNERS

Those whose main support comes from a few big "sugar daddies" may be in trouble when the economy tanks. For you, spread out to different cities and states, seeking to add a steady flow of new givers, even if they're just $50, $75, or $100 a month gifts. Creating a broader base of 100 monthly donors provides so much more long-term stability than hanging your hopes on five big hitters promising to tithe from their end-of-the-year real estate deals. And studies show people are less likely to cut back on a monthly commitment they have made to an individual Christian worker than they are a general gift to a church or charity.

4. FOCUS ON ESSENTIALS, NOT ELECTIVES

Kill your debt. Don't take on any new debt. Build up your savings account. Repair stuff rather than replace. Get creative. Plant a garden. Pool the whole family's incomes and expenses. Work together, and just like your struggling supporters, prayerfully distinguish between your *wants* and your *needs*.

5. EMPATHIZE WITH YOUR SUPPORTERS

Acknowledge to your givers the economy is suffering and they may have been affected. Ask what you can pray for them about. Be sensitive to their losses and pressures, never demanding they give, but with appreciation and humility asking them to continue to invest in God's work through you. During these tough times, Ellis and Colleen Goldstein with Cru have committed to pray for different supporters each night and then sending them a postcard telling them they did so.

6. KEEP THE MINISTRY VISION CENTRAL

Scott Morton with the Navigators says, "We must remember we are inviting supporters to advance the Kingdom, not merely to meet our personal needs."

YWAM's John Ray adds, "Let's help our supporters process what is really valuable and how their investments cannot be affected by the stock market or economy."

Finally, veteran fundraising consultant Bill McConkey says, "We should all be making Jesus the Lord of our asset base so it goes into the Kingdom *now*, and when we get to heaven God won't have to ask us why we were such hoarders!"

ADVICE FOR CHRISTIAN WORKERS

Advice from laymen around the U.S. who give:

MARK (CALIFORNIA) IN REAL ESTATE FINANCING

"Keep out of debt. Don't fall into the materialistic trap that plagues many Christians. Reach a broader support base to get a larger number of gifts. Reduce your lifestyle and keep costs down. God wants us to have daily bread and trust in Him, not a fat bank account!"

CLAY (ARKANSAS) IN MARKETING SERVICES

"I encourage support raisers to engage their donors and walk with them through these difficult times. Directing them to the Lord and the promise of honoring Him with their first fruits applies during prosperous and tough times. Ask: How am I adding value to the givers beyond just taking their gift?"

SCOTT (TEXAS) IN TECHNOLOGY SALES

"Christian workers need to help givers think BIG. Our vision is way too small and focused on what I have and what I need. Our God, who holds the future, has grand plans and it's exciting to be a part. Help us keep that in focus."

LANCE (FLORIDA) IN REAL ESTATE MANAGEMENT

"Communicate in simple ways what your ministry is about and how our gifts are being invested. We want our funds to be impactful, so give us a sense our gift (whether it's $100 or $1K a month) is very important."

JAY (KANSAS) A CORPORATE ATTORNEY

"Remember, God is the Great Provider and will make available the funds necessary to carry on His work. Cultivate relationships with your support team, helping them feel connected and responsible for the great results happening with the ministry."

ADVICE FROM CHRISTIAN MINISTRY LEADERS

DREW PEDERSON WITH EFCA REACHGLOBAL

"Churches are facing grim economic realities, and many are cutting support for missionaries. Primarily approaching churches will not be the 'preferred option to be the major source of financial support for our accepted candidates.' Our candidates need to know their audience, be prayerfully aware of their economic difficulties, but not be apologetic in their asking."

ED LOCHMOELLER WITH AMERICAN MISSIONARY FELLOWSHIP

"I keep stressing the need to share the vision and build relationships 'face to face.' We are overwhelmed that God has been increasing our support levels as a result."

GEORGE LORING WITH MISSIONS DOOR

"We are seeing those missionaries who have done a good job communicating and keeping up with their supporters actually increase their support by 17 percent. Those who have not are slipping in support."

64

FOUR STEPS TO BECOMING THE TIM TEBOW OF YOUR ORGANIZATION

W hether you follow college sports or not, I have to believe the name Tim Tebow is familiar to you. He is the home-schooled son of missionary parents who grew up playing football in small-town Florida, only to rise to the pinnacle of success as the quarterback of perennial powerhouse, the Florida Gators. Not only did Tebow lead his team to two NCAA championships, he also won the Heisman trophy (given to the most valuable college football player in the country), all kinds of other awards and accolades, and of course smashed numerous records along the way.

But it wasn't his records or trophies that set him apart from the other 2,000-plus college quarterbacks across the country; rather it was the profound influence he's had on his team, his coaches, his university, and millions of fans around the world. How did this toothy-grinned 21-year-old gee-whiz-of-a-kid with a crew cut straight from the 1950s capture the attention of the sports world, making us all sit up and take notice?

It appears Tebow's turning point may have come 60 minutes after unranked Ole Miss upset the mighty Gators 31-30 in front of a Gainesville, Florida home crowd on September 27, 2008. After grieving and praying at his locker for over an hour, he stormed into the post-game press conference and with tears in his eyes declared: "I'm sorry, extremely sorry. We were looking for an undefeated season. That was my goal. But I promise you one thing: A lot of good will come out of this. You have never seen any player in the entire country play as hard as I will play the rest of the season, and you will never see someone push the rest of the team as hard as I will push everybody the rest of the season. You'll never see a team play harder than we will the rest of the season. God bless." He bowed his head and walked out.

Those were not just empty promises spewed after an emotional loss. That was the day Tebow turned from a boy into a man, determined to single-handedly carry that whole team on his shoulders right through to the final whistle of the National Championship game. And that is exactly what he did. Although just one player, his resolute attitude and unbridled passion wielded more influence than the athletic director, all of the coaches, players, and sportswriters combined. Technically, he had no official authority or power, but it was obvious to all *who* the heart and soul of "Gator Nation" was — the humble, yet fiery Tim Tebow: Unpaid, unpretentious, undesignated leader of the pack.

This is a great example of what author John Maxwell calls "leading from the middle." We deceive ourselves into thinking we *can't* lead or bring about change in our organization unless some big title like "President" or "Director" is bestowed upon us from on high. Maxwell disagrees and states, "Leadership is influence — nothing more, nothing less." So, instead of wasting time jockeying for that promotion or corner office, why not begin now making a real difference in those around you? And just as Tebow did publicly, could we not also each make a private vow that we will make whatever sacrifice is required to help the people and programs of our ministry succeed? Regardless of how low on the totem pole you may be, here are four quick steps from the life of Tim Tebow to get you started:

- Give away credit for successes; accept responsibility for failures.
- View every setback as an opportunity to learn and improve.
- Be a pacesetter by modeling servanthood and hard work.
- Keep the big-picture goal clearly in focus for you and others.

65

HELPS TO CULTIVATE YOUR RELATIONSHIP WITH GOD

THE GOD YOU CAN KNOW BY DAN DEHAAN

DeHaan, a teacher and author, helps believers comprehend the person of God the Father and how He sees us and relates to us as His children. Burdened by contemporary Christians' lack of understanding of the nature of Almighty God, he wrote this book to help readers become intimate with God by studying His character and attributes.

FIRST LOVE: RENEWING YOUR PASSION FOR GOD BY BILL BRIGHT

Bright, the founder of Cru, refers us back to the Revelation passage describing believers as losing their "first love." In a first person discussion between the author and reader, Bright shares a heart-to-heart talk on how the Holy Spirit is a very real person in the daily life of the believer and is the only source of strength for maintaining our first love.

THE PURSUIT OF HOLINESS BY JERRY BRIDGES

Bridges, a long-time Navigator staffer, helps us see that holiness is not perfection, but mainly consists of effort, prayer, grace, and obedience. "Scripture speaks of both a holiness we have in Christ before God, and a holiness we are to strive after," writes the author. In other words, we can ignore neither Christ's role nor our own if we are to successfully pursue holiness.

KNOWLEDGE OF THE HOLY BY A.W. TOZER

Tozer, a Chicago pastor and author, preached and wrote on the character of God in powerful ways. He wanted believers to recapture a real sense of God's majesty and truly live in the Spirit. This classic focuses on 22 different attributes of God, showing us how we can rejuvenate our prayer life, meditate more reverently, understand God more deeply, and experience the Lord's presence in our daily lives.

DON'T WASTE YOUR LIFE BY JOHN PIPER

Piper, a pastor and prophet, believes that most people slip by in life without a passion for God, spending their lives on trivial diversions, living for comfort and pleasure, and perhaps trying to avoid sin. This book warns you not to get caught up in a life that counts for nothing, challenging you to live and die boasting in the cross of Christ and making the glory of God your singular passion.

EVANGELISM

PREPARE YOUR STUDENTS TO SHARE THE GOSPEL
EVERY MOMENT, EVERY DAY.

DISCIPLE MAKING

YOUR STUDENTS CAN
REPRODUCE GREAT LEADERS.

MISSION MOBILIZATION

GOD HAS BROUGHT THE NATIONS TO YOU.
PREPARE YOUR STUDENTS FOR GLOBAL IMPACT.

SHAPING THE LEADERSHIP OF COLLEGE MINISTRY

CAMPUS MINISTRY
JOURNAL

JOIN THE CONVERSATION

campusministrytoolbox.org

facebook.com/CampusMinistryToolbox

twitter.com/CMToolbox

BE SPIRITUALLY HEALTHY
VISION-DRIVEN &
FULLY FUNDED

**With staff from more than 500 organizations
trained, Support Raising Solutions is equipped
to help you get to your ministry assignment
quickly and fully funded.**

Explore these six resources and see how we can help
you thrive in the work that God has called you to. ⟶

 Support Raising
Solutions

Support Raising Solutions is a ministry of the Center for
Mission Mobilization. Learn more at mobilization.org.

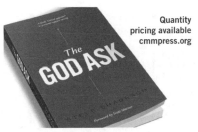

SRS Newsletter

The SRS Newsletter is helping thousands of ministry workers like you stay fully funded.

SUBSCRIBE HERE SupportRaisingSolutions.org

. . . .

SRS Newsletter Authors

BETTY BARNETT
YWAM

ELLIS GOLDSTEIN
Cru

SCOTT MORTON
The Navigators

MIKE RIGGINS
North American
Mission Board

STEVE SHADRACH
SRS Editor
Center for Mission
Mobilization

 facebook.com/supportraisingsolutions

 twitter.com/SupportRaising

ABOUT THE AUTHOR

Dr. Steve Shadrach founded the ministries of Student Mobilization and The Traveling Team. For years, he was the Director of Mobilization for the U.S. Center for World Mission, overseeing the Perspectives on the World Christian Movement program across the U.S. and world. He is the Executive Director of the Center for Mission Mobilization (formerly known as The BodyBuilders) which sponsors the SRS Bootcamps and Support Raising Solutions resources. He has trained thousands of Christian workers from over 500 organizations around the world how to launch their ministries and raise their support. A former pastor and missionary himself, he has a Doctorate of Ministry in Church and Para-Church Executive Leadership. He and his wife Carol and five children (and three grandchildren!) reside in Fayetteville, Arkansas and have lived and ministered on support since 1986.

Ministries Steve Shadrach serves:
- Student Mobilization (Stumo.org)
- The Traveling Team (TheTravelingTeam.org)
- Perspectives on the World Christian Movement (Perspectives.org)
- Every Ethne Collegiate Mobilizers (EveryEthne.org)
- Support Raising Solutions (SupportRaisingSolutions.org)
- Campus Ministry Toolbox (CMTBox.org)
- SevenNine International Mission Mobilization (79Online.org)
- CMM Press (CMMPress.org)
- Center for Mission Mobilization (Mobilization.org)